anne frank

anne frank

THE ANNE FRANK HOUSE
AUTHORIZED
GRAPHIC BIOGRAPHY

SID JACOBSON AND ERNIE COLÓN

A Novel Graphic from Hill and Wang
A division of Farrar, Straus and Giroux
NEW YORK

This graphic biography was developed by the authors for Hill and Wang, a division of Farrar, Straus and Giroux, 18 West 18th Street, New York 10011, in collaboration with the Anne Frank House of Amsterdam, the Netherlands

Distributed in Canada by D&M Publishers, Inc.
Printed in the United States of America
Published simultaneously in hardcover and paperback
First edition, 2010

Library of Congress Cataloging-in-Publication Data
Jacobson, Sidney.
    Anne Frank : the Anne Frank House authorized graphic biography / Sid Jacobson and Ernie
Colón. — 1st ed.
        p. cm.
    "A novel graphic from Hill and Wang."
    Includes bibliographical references.
    ISBN: 978-0-8090-2684-5 (hardcover : alk. paper)
    ISBN: 978-0-8090-2685-2 (pbk. : alk. paper)
    1. Frank, Anne, 1929–1945—Comic books, strips, etc. 2. Jewish children in the
Holocaust—Netherlands—Amsterdam—Biography—Comic books, strips, etc. 3. Jews—
Netherlands—Amsterdam—Biography—Comic books, strips, etc. 4. Holocaust, Jewish
(1939–1945)—Netherlands—Amsterdam—Biography—Comic books, strips, etc.
5. Amsterdam (Netherlands)—Biography—Comic books, strips, etc. 6. Graphic novels.
I. Colón, Ernie. II. Anne Frank House. III. Title.

DS135.N6F73357 2010
940.53'18092—dc22
[B]
                                                                    2010005776

www.fsgbooks.com

1 3 5 7 9 10 8 6 4 2

I would like to dedicate this book to my children, Seth and Kathy, who but for the fortune of time and place could have suffered the tragic fate of the young sisters you are about to meet.

—SID JACOBSON

Watching my daughters grow into young women gave me a deep sense of what Anne Frank and her sister Margot missed and what a loss they were to us all. This one is for Amanda, Luisa, and Rebecca.

—ERNIE COLÓN

CONTENTS

anne frank

CHAPTER 1
A Hopeful Beginning

EDITH AND OTTO FRANK, ON THEIR WEDDING DAY, MAY 12, 1925, IN AACHEN, GERMANY

"HAVE I EVER TOLD YOU ANYTHING ABOUT OUR FAMILY?" ANNE FRANK ASKED HER DIARY ON MAY 8, 1944.

"MY FATHER WAS BORN IN FRANKFURT AM MAIN." OTTO FRANK WAS BORN ON MAY 12, 1889.

"FATHER LIVED THE LIFE OF A RICH MAN'S SON," ANNE WENT ON.

MAY I HAVE THIS DANCE?

IT WOULD BE A PLEASURE, OTTO.

OTTO AND HIS BROTHERS, HERBERT AND ROBERT, AND HIS SISTER, LENI, CERTAINLY DID LIVE PRIVILEGED LIVES, SO LONG AS THE MICHAEL FRANK BANK, WHICH SPECIALIZED IN THE EXCHANGE OF FOREIGN MONEY, PROSPERED.

ABOUT HER MOTHER'S FAMILY, ANNE WROTE: "WE'VE LISTENED OPENMOUTHED TO STORIES OF PRIVATE BALLS, DINNER AND ENGAGEMENT PARTIES WITH 250 GUESTS."

EDITH!

SO SORRY I'M LATE...

EDITH'S FAMILY HAD MIGRATED FROM THE NETHERLANDS (THUS THEIR NAME, HOLLÄNDER) IN THE 18TH CENTURY AND LIVED IN AACHEN, GERMANY, CLOSE TO THE DUTCH BORDER.

THE HOLLÄNDERS WERE OBSERVANT JEWS, UNLIKE THE MORE LIBERAL FRANKS.

4

THESE ARE THE FRANK AND
HOLLÄNDER FAMILY TREES

*NO PHOTOGRAPH AVAILABLE

5

OTTO AND HIS BROTHERS, HERBERT AND ROBERT, SERVED IN THE ARMY.

I AM SO PROUD OF YOU, MY SONS.

JULIUS HOLLÄNDER, EDITH'S BROTHER, ALSO SERVED DURING WORLD WAR I.

ABOUT 96,000 JEWISH SOLDIERS FOUGHT FOR GERMANY IN WORLD WAR I. TWELVE THOUSAND OF THEM WERE KILLED, 21,000 WERE PROMOTED TO OFFICER, AND 35,000 WERE DECORATED.

IN NOVEMBER 1917, OTTO'S ARTILLERY REGIMENT WAS CLOSE TO THE ACTION IN THE FIRST GREAT TANK BATTLE IN HISTORY, NEAR CAMBRAI IN NORTHERN FRANCE.

ARE YOU MORE COMFORTABLE NOW?

OTTO'S MOTHER, ALICE, AND HIS SISTER, LENI, BOTH WORKED AS VOLUNTEER NURSES.

IN 1918, OTTO WAS PROMOTED TO LIEUTENANT AND AWARDED THE IRON CROSS SECOND CLASS FOR HIS SERVICE.

YES, NURSE LENI, THANK YOU.

SNAPSHOT: GERMANY IN WORLD WAR I
OTTO AND HIS BROTHERS WERE LUCKY. HIS FRENCH COUSINS GEORGES-OTTMAR AND OSCAR FRANK WEREN'T.

THEY BOTH WERE KILLED IN 1915. MILLIONS DIED DURING WORLD WAR I. WHAT CAUSED THIS BLOODSHED?

THE IMMEDIATE CAUSE OF WORLD WAR I (1914–1918) WAS THE KILLING OF ARCHDUKE FRANZ FERDINAND OF AUSTRIA, AND HIS WIFE, SOPHIE, IN SARAJEVO, BOSNIA, ON JUNE 28, 1914, BY SERBIAN ASSASSINS.

AUSTRIA-HUNGARY RESPONDED BY DECLARING WAR ON SERBIA. GERMANY QUICKLY FOLLOWED AND TOOK THE LEAD. THEN A SERIES OF EUROPEAN ALLIANCES RAPIDLY TURNED THE CONFLICT INTO A WORLD WAR.

AMERICA JOINED THE ALLIED POWERS ON APRIL 6, 1917.

EUROPE 1914

NORWAY
SWEDEN
DENMARK
ENGLAND
NETH.
GERMANY
BELGIUM
LUX.
RUSSIA
FRANCE
SWITZ.
AUSTRIA-HUNGARY
ITALY
RUMANIA
SERBIA
BULGARIA
PORTUGAL
SPAIN
ALBANIA
GREECE
OTTOMAN EMPIRE
SPANISH MOROCCO

ALLIES
CENTRAL POWERS
NEUTRAL NATIONS

THE WAR ENDED IN THE DEFEAT OF GERMANY AND ITS ALLIES, AND AN ARMISTICE WAS SIGNED IN A RAILWAY CAR ON NOVEMBER 11, 1918.

MORE THAN 9 MILLION SOLDIERS WERE KILLED AND 21 MILLION WERE WOUNDED IN COMBAT INFAMOUSLY DEFINED BY TRENCH WARFARE. MILES UPON MILES OF TRENCHES CONFRONTED EACH OTHER ACROSS A WASTED NO-MAN'S-LAND, A STALEMATE THAT WEAPONS SUCH AS POISON GAS AND MACHINE GUNS DID NOT ALTER.

THE PEACE TREATY OF VERSAILLES WAS SIGNED ON JUNE 28, 1919, SIX MONTHS AFTER OTTO FRANK RETURNED HOME. PARTS OF GERMANY WERE CEDED TO VICTORIOUS NATIONS, OTHER SECTIONS WERE DEMILITARIZED, AND THE IMPOSED REPARATIONS PROVED RUINOUS TO ITS ALREADY STRAINED ECONOMY, SOWING THE SEEDS OF BITTERNESS AND RESENTMENT FOR MANY GERMANS.

10

AFTER RETURNING FROM THEIR HONEYMOON, OTTO AND EDITH MOVED IN WITH OTTO'S WIDOWED MOTHER IN HER SPACIOUS AND ELEGANT HOME IN THE FASHIONABLE WEST END OF FRANKFURT...

WHEN WILL WE HAVE A PLACE OF OUR OWN?

...WHERE THEY LIVED FOR TWO YEARS.

ON JULY 18, 1925, ADOLF HITLER PUBLISHED THE FIRST VOLUME OF HIS AUTOBIOGRAPHY, MEIN KAMPF (MY STRUGGLE). AT THE TIME, HE WAS THE LEADER OF A SMALL POLITICAL PARTY, THE NSDAP (NATIONAL SOCIALIST PARTY).

HE AND HIS SUPPORTERS (WHO WERE CALLED NAZIS) BLAMED THE JEWS IN GERMANY FOR THE LOSS OF WORLD WAR I AND FOR ALL OTHER PROBLEMS THE NATION FACED.

ON FEBRUARY 16, 1926, THE FRANKS' FIRST DAUGHTER, MARGOT BETTI, WAS BORN. MARGOT SLEPT THROUGH THE NIGHT IMMEDIATELY...

IN 1927, THE FRANK FAMILY MOVED INTO THEIR OWN APARTMENT AT 307 MARBACHWEG, IN A NEW DISTRICT OF FRANKFURT.

...AND RARELY CRIED.

ON MAY 28, 1928, THE NSDAP WON 2.6% OF THE REICHSTAG VOTE AND THUS WON 12 OF THE 491 SEATS OF THE GERMAN REPUBLIC'S LEGISLATIVE BODY.

11

THREE-YEAR-OLD MARGOT WAS QUICKLY A FAVORITE OF HILDE STAAB AND GERTRUD NAUMANN, OLDER CHILDREN OF NEIGHBORING CATHOLIC FAMILIES WHO FOUND HER AN EASY CHILD TO BABYSIT.

THEN, ON JUNE 11, 1929...

OTTO, OTTO! IT'S TIME.

EDITH FRANK, IN HER NINTH MONTH OF PREGNANCY...

BE CALM, MY DARLING, YOU'RE GOING TO BE ALL RIGHT.

...WAS RUSHED TO THE HOSPITAL FOR AN IMPENDING BIRTH.

CHAPTER 2

Annelies Marie Frank

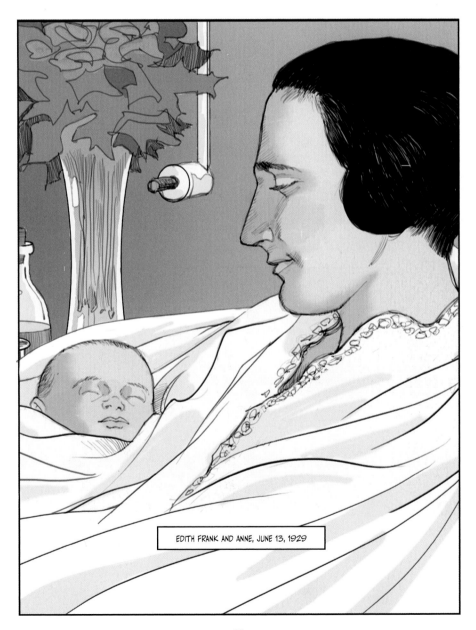

EDITH FRANK AND ANNE, JUNE 13, 1929

ANNELIES MARIE FRANK WAS BORN AT 7:30 IN THE MORNING OF JUNE 12, 1929. SHE WEIGHED 9.1 POUNDS AND WAS 21.25 INCHES LONG.

TWO DAYS LATER, GRANDMA HOLLÄNDER AND MARGOT CAME TO VISIT.

EDITH, ANNE IS ADORABLE.

MUMMY, CAN I HOLD HER? PLEASE?

ANNE, HOWEVER, WAS NOT A QUIET BABY. STOMACHACHES AND A HEAT WAVE KEPT HER, AND EDITH, UP.

"AT NIGHT FOR SIX WEEKS, SHE CRIES A LOT," EDITH WROTE IN ANNE'S BABY PHOTO ALBUM.

SHE COULD ALSO CHARM.

AS EDITH OBSERVED, SHE "SMILES AT PAPA."

AND SHE'S SMILING AT YOU.

15

16

17

CHAPTER 3

The Growth of Nazism

SNAPSHOT: THE RISE AND APPEAL OF THE NAZI PARTY

THE GERMAN WORKERS PARTY WAS A SMALL, INSIGNIFICANT POLITICAL PARTY. ADOLF HITLER JOINED IT IN 1919 AND BECAME ITS LEADER IN 1921. IN 1920 ITS NAME WAS CHANGED TO NATIONAL SOCIALIST GERMAN WORKERS PARTY (NSDAP, OR THE NAZI PARTY).

NSDAP

THEIR 25-POINT PROGRAM CALLED FOR ABOLISHING THE VERSAILLES PEACE TREATY, THE UNIFICATION OF ALL ETHNIC GERMANS, GREATER TERRITORY FOR GERMANY, AND CITIZEN RIGHTS FOR GERMANS ONLY.

(THE NAZIS DID NOT CONSIDER JEWS TO BE GERMANS)

THE CHARISMATIC LEADERSHIP OF ADOLF HITLER AND GERMANY'S DETERIORATING ECONOMIC CONDITIONS CAUSED MORE AND MORE PEOPLE TO VOTE FOR THE NAZI PARTY.

Arbeiter erwacht!

liſte 2 Nationalſozialiſten

deutſchland erwacht! Nationalſozialiſten 2

WÄHLT BRÜNING DEUTSCHE ZENTRUMS- PARTEI 4

Freiheit! 1 liste SOZIALDEMOKRATEN

IN THE 1932 ELECTIONS, THE NSDAP BECAME THE LARGEST PARTY IN THE GERMAN PARLIAMENT.

23

ON JANUARY 30, 1933, OTTO AND EDITH WERE AT AN ACQUAINTANCE'S HOME WHEN THEY HEARD ON THE RADIO:

"HITLER HAS BECOME CHANCELLOR."

"THERE IS A TORCH PARADE OF STORM TROOPERS."

"HITLER IS STANDING AT THE WINDOW, WAVING..."

"...TO CROWDS OF CHEERING, CELEBRATING BERLINERS."

THEIR HOST THEN SAID ENTHUSIASTICALLY...

LET'S SEE WHAT THAT MAN CAN DO!

24

UNDER CONTINUED FINANCIAL STRESS, IN MARCH THE FRANKS DECIDED TO MOVE INTO OTTO'S MOTHER'S HOUSE.

WE'LL HAVE MUCH MORE ROOM.

AND YOUR GRANDMOTHER WILL LOVE YOUR COMPANY.

JUST DAYS BEFORE, ON THE NIGHT OF FEBRUARY 27, 1933, A SUSPICIOUS FIRE BROKE OUT IN THE REICHSTAG BUILDING. THE NAZIS BLAMED THE COMMUNISTS, PASSED OPPRESSIVE LAWS, AND KILLED, ARRESTED, AND TORTURED THE GERMANS WHO ROSE IN OPPOSITION, PLACING MANY IN CONCENTRATION CAMPS SUCH AS DACHAU AND ORANIENBURG.

DEM DEUTSCHEN VOLKE

WHEN THE FRANKS MOVED, THEIR PLANS TO LEAVE GERMANY WERE ALREADY FORMING. AS TO WHERE, THEY DID NOT YET KNOW.

WE MUST FIND A WAY TO LEAVE GERMANY.

YES, IT'S BECOMING TOO DANGEROUS.

IN FULL CONTROL OF THE GOVERNMENT, THE NAZIS QUICKLY PUT THEIR IDEAS INTO ACTION:

*THE FEBRUARY 28 REICHSTAG FIRE DECREE ABOLISHED CONSTITUTIONAL RIGHTS AND ALLOWED INDEFINITE DETENTION WITHOUT WARRANTS.
*THE FIRST CONCENTRATION CAMP, IN DACHAU, WAS ESTABLISHED ON MARCH 22.
*ON MARCH 23, THE "ENABLING ACT" PASSED, MAKING HITLER THE NATION'S DICTATOR.
*ON APRIL 1, A BOYCOTT OF JEWISH DOCTORS, LAWYERS, SHOPS, AND DEPARTMENT STORES WAS ENACTED.
*AS OF APRIL 7, JEWISH CIVIL SERVANTS AND ANYONE OPPOSING THE NEW GOVERNMENT COULD BE SUMMARILY FIRED.
*THOUSANDS OF BOOKS DEEMED "UN-GERMAN" BY THE NAZIS WERE BURNED IN BERLIN AND OTHER CITIES ON MAY 10.

OTTO'S BROTHER-IN-LAW, ERICH ELIAS, IN BASEL HAD AN IDEA AS TO WHERE THE FRANKS COULD EMIGRATE.

ERICH BELIEVES HE CAN GET ME A POSITION WITH HIS FIRM IN THE NETHERLANDS.

IT WON'T BE EASY. I WILL MISS FRANKFURT.

OTTO, WHO HAD DONE BUSINESS IN THE NETHERLANDS IN 1923-24, FELT IT WOULD BE A GOOD OPPORTUNITY.

THROUGH ERICH, HE MET WITH OPEKTA.

I KNOW AMSTERDAM...

WE EXPECT YOU TO SELL PECTIN IN THE DUTCH MARKET.

...AND ERICH HAS TOLD ME ALL ABOUT PECTIN AND ITS USE IN MAKING JAM.

THEY WERE WILLING TO TAKE THE CHANCE...

ERICH SPEAKS THAT HIGHLY OF YOU.

OF COURSE I WILL LEND YOU THE START-UP CAPITAL.

I AM SO GRATEFUL!

HOW CAN I EVER REPAY YOU?

OTTO, WITH THE AID OF ERICH, WOULD ESTABLISH HIS OWN COMPANY TO SELL OPEKTA PECTIN TO DUTCH PRIVATE CONSUMERS EXCLUSIVELY, THE ONE REMAINING AVAILABLE MARKET.

SHORTLY AFTERWARD, THEY TOLD MARGOT AND ANNE...

WE ARE GOING TO MOVE...

ISN'T THAT EXCITING?

SOON ALL THE FRANKS WOULD LEAVE FRANKFURT, A CITY IN WHICH THE FAMILY HAD LIVED FOR CENTURIES. HERBERT LEFT FOR PARIS IN THE SUMMER OF 1932. ROBERT AND LOTTI WENT TO LONDON IN THE MIDDLE OF 1933.

AND MOTHER ALICE LEFT FOR BASEL IN OCTOBER 1933 TO JOIN LENI AND ERICH ELIAS.

CHAPTER 4

Amsterdam

WHILE OTTO PUT TOGETHER HIS NEW BUSINESS IN AMSTERDAM, EDITH BROUGHT THE GIRLS TO OMA HOLLÄNDER IN AACHEN.

I HOPE I'LL FIND A NICE APARTMENT IN AMSTERDAM, MOTHER.

YES DEAR, I'LL KEEP MY FINGERS CROSSED...

IT TOOK TIME, BUT AFTER MANY DAYS OF SEARCHING...

IT'S A LOT SMALLER THAN OUR PLACE IN GANGHOFERSTRASSE.

BUT I THINK IT WILL WORK FOR US, SWEETHEART.

ON DECEMBER 5, 1933, OTTO AND EDITH MOVED INTO THE APARTMENT...

THE GIRLS WILL LOVE IT HERE.

...AT 37 MERWEDEPLEIN IN A NEWLY BUILT NEIGHBORHOOD IN THE SOUTH OF AMSTERDAM.

WE CAN MAKE A NEW START HERE.

NO CELLAR, NO ATTIC, BUT EVERYTHING IS BRIGHT AND WARM.

THE FRANKS' NEIGHBORHOOD WAS NEWLY BUILT AND MADE UP OF RELATIVELY EXPENSIVE HOMES. IT WOULD EVENTUALLY CONTAIN 50,000 PEOPLE, ONE-THIRD OF WHOM WERE JEWS, MANY OF THEM FROM NAZI GERMANY

OTTO AND EDITH OPENED THEIR HOME TO THEIR MANY NEW ACQUAINTANCES, INCLUDING THE GOSLARS AND THE LEDERMANNS.

HANS GOSLAR AND FRANZ LEDERMANN WERE ACTIVELY INVOLVED IN HELPING REFUGEES FROM NAZI GERMANY.

YOU REMAIN BUSY?

VERY!

MORE AND MORE REFUGEES NEED OUR HELP...

SUSANNE LEDERMANN, THE DAUGHTER OF FRANZ AND ILSE, ALSO BECAME FRIENDS WITH ANNE AND HANNELI.

HELLO, ANNE, HANNE, AND SANNE.

SHE CALLED US ANNE, HANNE, AND SANNE.

I LIKE IT!

A RHYME TO SKIP TO!

36

37

SNAPSHOT: NUREMBERG LAWS

ON SEPTEMBER 15, 1935, THE REICHSTAG MET IN NUREMBERG TO COINCIDE WITH A NAZI PARTY RALLY. THAT EVENING, HERMANN GÖRING, AS PRESIDENT OF THE REICHSTAG, PROCLAIMED THE NUREMBERG LAWS, WHICH TOOK AWAY FUNDAMENTAL RIGHTS OF JEWS IN GERMANY.

THESE LAWS SECURE OUR FREEDOM INSIDE AND OUTSIDE AND LAY THE FOUNDATION FOR THE RISE OF OUR PEOPLE.

THE CITIZEN LAW DISTINGUISHED BETWEEN "CITIZENS OF THE REICH," WHO WERE GIVEN FULL POLITICAL AND CIVIL RIGHTS, AND "SUBJECTS," WHO WERE ENTITLED TO NONE. INDIVIDUALS WITH "GERMAN OR RELATED BLOOD," SO-CALLED ARYANS, WERE CITIZENS. JEWS FELL INTO THE SECOND GROUP.

FILTHY JEW!

NICHT FÜR JUDEN

WHAT CAN I DO?

THE LAW FOR THE DEFENSE OF GERMAN BLOOD AND HONOR FORBADE JEWS AND GERMANS TO MARRY OR HAVE EXTRAMARITAL SEX. JEWS WERE ALSO FORBIDDEN TO HIRE FEMALE GERMAN HOUSEKEEPERS LESS THAN 45 YEARS OF AGE.

ANYONE WITH ONE QUARTER JEWISH HERITAGE OR MORE WAS CONSIDERED JEWISH.

AND THE REICH FLAG LAW HENCEFORTH MADE THE GERMAN NATIONAL COLORS BLACK, RED, AND WHITE, AND THE SWASTIKA, SYMBOL OF THE NAZI PARTY, THE NATIONAL FLAG.

TOGETHER, THE LAWS FURTHER ISOLATED GERMAN JEWS. FEW GERMANS PROTESTED.

UNLIKE OPEKTA, IT HAS A YEAR-ROUND DEMAND, OTTO

I SEE YOUR POINT, JO.

HERMANN, YOU'VE CONVINCED ME!

IN LATE 1938, OTTO, TOGETHER WITH HIS OLD FRIEND JOHANNES KLEIMAN AND HERMANN VAN PELS, STARTED A NEW COMPANY, PECTACON...

...WHICH SOLD SPICES FOR SAUSAGES AND MEATS.

OTTO HAD KNOWN KLEIMAN SINCE 1923, WHEN THEY HAD TRIED--UNSUCCESSFULLY--TO ESTABLISH AN AMSTERDAM BRANCH OF THE MICHAEL FRANK BANK.

WE'VE COME A LONG WAY FROM BANKING, MY OLD FRIEND.

PECTIN AND SPICES...

THE VAN PELS FAMILY WAS JEWISH. HERMANN VAN PELS, A DUTCHMAN WHO HAD GROWN UP IN GERMANY, RETURNED TO THE NETHERLANDS WITH HIS WIFE, AUGUSTE, AND SON, PETER, IN 1937.

I AM SURE THIS WILL WORK, TRUST ME. I AM A SPICE SPECIALIST...

BY 1938, HITLER HAD REPEATEDLY TESTED EUROPE'S RESPONSE TO AN INCREASINGLY MILITANT GERMANY, WHICH HAD...

*STARTED MILITARY CONSCRIPTION ON MARCH 16, 1935

*REOCCUPIED THE RHINELAND ON MARCH 7, 1936

*DECLARED THE VERSAILLES TREATY INVALID ON JANUARY 30, 1937

*AND ON MARCH 12, 1938, ENTERED VIENNA AND ANNEXED AUSTRIA

41

MY FORMER HUSBAND AND SON ARE STILL IN BERLIN...

WE WERE VERY LUCKY TO GET WERNER TO ENGLAND.

IN THE MONTHS PRIOR TO WAR, ENGLAND WOULD TAKE IN 10,000 REFUGEES, ALL CHILDREN, MOST JEWS FROM NAZI GERMANY.

"I TOOK HIM TO BREMERHAVEN, WHERE HE BOARDED A SHIP TO SOUTHAMPTON."

TAKE CARE, WERNER, AND DON'T WORRY ABOUT US.

THAT WAS SOON AFTER KRISTALLNACHT...

THAT TERRIBLE NIGHT...

SNAPSHOT: KRISTALLNACHT HERSCHEL GRYNSZPAN WAS AN IMPOVERISHED 17-YEAR-OLD POLISH JEW. HIS FAMILY-- LIKE 17,000 OTHERS--HAD BEEN DEPORTED TO POLAND FROM THEIR HOME IN GERMANY.

HERSCHEL LIVED IN PARIS AND BECAME DESPERATE...

BLAM!

ON NOVEMBER 7, 1938, HE ENTERED THE GERMAN EMBASSY AND SHOT AND FATALLY WOUNDED ERNST VOM RATH, AN OFFICIAL THERE.

42

USING THIS KILLING AS A PRETEXT, ON NOVEMBER 9 AND 10 THE NAZIS ORGANIZED A POGROM, WHICH THEY CLAIMED WAS A "SPONTANEOUS" DISPLAY OF "POPULAR ANGER." THOUSANDS OF SYNAGOGUES AND JEWISH HOMES AND SHOPS WERE RANSACKED. MORE THAN 100 JEWS WERE MURDERED, AND MORE THAN 30,000 WERE INCARCERATED IN CONCENTRATION CAMPS. AFTER KRISTALLNACHT, OR THE "NIGHT OF BROKEN GLASS," NAZI ARYANIZATION, ISOLATING JEWS ECONOMICALLY AND PHYSICALLY, INCREASED RAPIDLY.

THE NAZIS BLAMED THE JEWS FOR THE POGROM AND FORCED THEM TO PAY FOR THE DAMAGE. A FINE OF ONE BILLION REICHSMARKS WAS IMPOSED ON THE COMMUNITY. THOUSANDS OF JEWS FLED GERMANY EVEN AS MANY COUNTRIES CLOSED THEIR BORDERS TO THE REFUGEES.

WE HAVEN'T HAD ANY NEWS FROM WERNER IN ENGLAND.

BUT WE HOPE AND WE PRAY FOR THE BEST.

43

AS THINGS GREW WORSE FOR JEWS IN GERMANY, THE HOLLÄNDERS FINALLY LEFT THE COUNTRY. EDITH'S BROTHER JULIUS, AFTER MUCH DIFFICULTY, GAINED ENTRY INTO THE U.S. IN 1939. HER BROTHER WALTER WAS ARRESTED DURING KRISTALLNACHT AND IMPRISONED IN A CONCENTRATION CAMP. HE WAS RELEASED ONLY WHEN HE PROMISED TO EMIGRATE AND AFTER HE SURRENDERED THE FAMILY FORTUNE TO NAZI AUTHORITIES. HE MANAGED TO GO TO THE NETHERLANDS AND WAS ALSO ALLOWED ENTRY INTO THE U.S.

AND ROSA HOLLÄNDER, AT THE AGE OF 72, MOVED IN WITH EDITH AND OTTO IN MARCH 1939. SHE HAD TO LEAVE EVERYTHING BEHIND.

WHERE JEWISH REFUGEES IMMIGRATED TO

NORWAY 2,000

SWEDEN 3,200

DENMARK 2,000

UK 52,000

POLAND 25,000

CANADA 6,000

GERMANY

SYRIA 3,000

CZECH. 5,000

USA 102,200

HUNGARY 3,000

FRANCE 30,000

SW. 7,000

ITALY 5,000

YUGO. 7,000

PORTUGAL 12,000

SOUTH AFRICA 26,100

SPAIN 3,000

URUGUAY- 20
BOLIVIA- 7,000
BRAZIL- 8,000

PALESTINE 33,400

VENEZUELA- 600
CARIBBEAN- 3,500
ARGENTINA- 63,500
SHANGHAI- 20,000

AUSTRALIA 8,800

BELGIUM 30,000
NETHERLANDS 30,000
JAPAN- SEVERAL HUNDRED

PHILIPPINES- 700

44

CHAPTER 5
Under German Rule

IN THE NETHERLANDS, THE FRANK FAMILY STILL ENJOYED THEIR FREEDOM. THEY SPENT THEIR SUMMER HOLIDAYS OF 1937 IN NEARBY BELGIUM AT THE SEASIDE RESORT OF MIDDELKERKE.

ANNE'S CLASSES AT THE MONTESSORI SCHOOL CONTINUED HAPPILY AND SUCCESSFULLY.

SHE OFTEN WALKED TO SCHOOL WITH HER TEACHER, MR. VAN GELDER, TELLING HIM POEMS AND STORIES THAT SHE AND HER FATHER HAD MADE UP TOGETHER.

...AND THEN THE PRINCESS WAS NO LONGER ALONE.

THAT'S THE END.

I THINK I WANT TO BE A WRITER, MR. VAN GELDER.

"I IMAGINE SHE MIGHT VERY WELL HAVE BECOME ONE," VAN GELDER COMMENTED YEARS LATER.

AROUND THIS TIME, EDITH ENJOYED TEACHING THE GIRLS TO KNIT AND TO EMBROIDER.

I'M GETTING IT!

EDITH AND MARGOT WENT TO THE LIBERAL SYNAGOGUE REGULARLY, WHILE...

DADDY AND ANNE NEVER SEEM TO WANT TO COME.

46

ANNE CELEBRATED HER TENTH BIRTHDAY ON JUNE 12, 1939, WITH EIGHT OF HER CLOSEST FRIENDS AND GAMES IN WHICH OTTO TOOK PART.

VERY MUCH THE SAME PRECOCIOUS CHILD, ANNE STILL WANTED HER OWN WAY IN EVERYTHING. HER FATHER HAD WRITTEN TO HER JUST A MONTH BEFORE, "WE HAVE AGREED THE 'CONTROLS' WITH EACH OTHER AND YOU YOURSELF ARE DOING A GREAT DEAL TO SWALLOW THE 'BUTS.'"

NOT UNTIL YOU FINISH YOUR HOMEWORK.

BUT...BUT I WANT TO GO NOW!

OTTO'S LETTER ALSO NOTED THAT "AFTER A FEW TEARS...

SHE'LL LEARN... SHE'S GOT TO LEARN!

"...THE LAUGHTER IS BACK...THE LAUGHTER WITH WHICH YOU ENHANCE YOUR, OUR, AND OTHER PEOPLES' LIVES."

I'LL GO FIRST!

IN RESPONSE TO GERMANY'S AGGRESSIVE FOREIGN POLICY, SOME NATIONS, SUCH AS BRITAIN AND FRANCE, SOUGHT TO APPEASE HITLER. OTHERS, LIKE THE NETHERLANDS, TRUSTED THAT THEIR NEUTRALITY WOULD BE RESPECTED.

ARE WE SAFE?

FOR NOW, I THINK YES. IF ONLY I COULD HAVE STARTED A BUSINESS IN ENGLAND.

THINGS GREW IMMENSELY WORSE IN AUGUST AND SEPTEMBER 1939.

ON SEPTEMBER 1, GERMANY INVADED POLAND. POLAND WAS DIVIDED BETWEEN GERMANY AND RUSSIA...

ON AUGUST 23, THE NAZIS SIGNED A NONAGGRESSION PACT WITH THE SOVIET UNION; THE TWO NATIONS AGREED TO SPHERES OF INFLUENCE IN FINLAND, ESTONIA, LATVIA, LITHUANIA, ROMANIA, AND POLAND.

OTTO'S SENSE OF SECURITY WAVERED, AND HE WROTE OF HIS WORRIES TO HIS COUSIN MILLY STANFIELD IN LONDON.

SHE OFFERS TO LOOK AFTER ANNE AND MARGOT.

...AND, ON SEPTEMBER 3, THIS CAUSED GREAT BRITAIN AND FRANCE TO DECLARE WAR ON GERMANY.

BUT, DARLING, THAT WOULD BE UNBEARABLE FOR US...

THEY JUST COULD NOT BEAR TO PART WITH THE GIRLS.

IN A LETTER TO BETTY ANN WAGNER, AN AMERICAN PEN PAL, IN APRIL 1940, MARGOT EXPRESSED HER OWN UNCERTAINTY...

"WE OFTEN LISTEN TO THE RADIO... HAVING A FRONTIER WITH GERMANY AND BEING A SMALL COUNTRY, WE NEVER FEEL SAFE."

"GERMAN FORCES ARE ADVANCING IN NORWAY..."

ANNE'S LETTER TO BETTY'S SISTER JUANITA, WHICH OTTO TRANSLATED INTO ENGLISH, KEPT TO LIGHTER SUBJECTS.

"...I AM INCLUDING A POSTCARD FROM AMSTERDAM...I ALREADY HAVE ABOUT 800."

I WILL SEND THE ONE WITH THE CANAL!

BUT THE CORRESPONDENCE WOULD END ABRUPTLY.

48

263 PRINSENGRACHT WAS A 300-YEAR-OLD BUILDING THAT SAT ALONGSIDE THE CANAL. THE WAREHOUSE WAS ON THE GROUND FLOOR, OFFICES ON THE SECOND, AND ADDITIONAL STORAGE ROOMS ON THE THIRD AND FOURTH.

PART OF THE ANNEX WAS SUBLET TO A PHARMACIST FRIEND OF OTTO'S NAMED ARTHUR LEWINSOHN. THE REMAINING ROOMS AND THE ATTIC OF THE ANNEX REMAINED EMPTY

ANNE WOULD OCCASIONALLY VISIT HER FATHER, SOMETIMES WITH HANNELI OR ANOTHER FRIEND, USING THE TELEPHONES, PLAYING WITH THE TYPEWRITERS,

MAY I SPEAK WITH MISS GOSLAR...

AND EVEN POURING WATER OUT THE WINDOWS.

I'LL BET I CAN TYPE FASTER THAN YOU...

BET NOT!

HEH HEH!

HUSH, HANNELI...

51

HER GIGGLE WAS SO INFECTIOUS, IT WAS DIFFICULT TO BE ANGRY AT HER PRANKS.

ANNE, THAT WAS SOMETHING YOU SHOULD NOT--

OH, I GIVE UP!

IN OCTOBER 1940, JEWISH BUSINESSES HAD TO REGISTER. IN ORDER TO KEEP HIS COMPANIES, OTTO TRANSFERRED HIS OWNERSHIP TO HIS LOYAL EMPLOYEES JOHANNES KLEIMAN AND VICTOR KUGLER, AND TO JAN GIES.

OF COURSE, HE SECRETLY REMAINED IN CHARGE.

THE NAZIS WON'T GET MY COMPANIES.

THE NAZIS SOON BEGAN A SERIES OF REPRESSIVE ORDINANCES TO ISOLATE THE JEWS. ONLY A FEW ARE LISTED HERE:

OCTOBER 5, 1940--ALL GOVERNMENT OFFICIALS MUST DECLARE WHETHER THEY ARE JEWISH OR NOT.
OCTOBER 22, 1940--BUSINESSES WITH MORE THAN 25% JEWISH OWNERSHIP HAVE TO REGISTER.
JANUARY 7, 1941--JEWS ARE NOT ALLOWED IN MOVIE THEATERS.
JANUARY 10, 1941--ALL JEWS IN NETHERLANDS MUST REGISTER.
APRIL 15, 1941--JEWS MUST HAND IN THEIR RADIOS.
MAY 31, 194--JEWS ARE BARRED FROM BEACHES, POOLS, PARKS, SPAS, AND HOTELS.

ZWEMBAD

Voor Joden verboden

IN EARLY 1941, DUTCH NAZIS PROVOKED FIGHTS WITH JEWS IN AMSTERDAM. WHEN ON FEBRUARY 11 A DUTCH NAZI WAS KILLED AND ON FEBRUARY 19 GERMAN POLICEMEN WERE ATTACKED, THE GERMAN POLICE RESPONDED BY ROUNDING UP 427 JEWISH MEN AND DEPORTING THEM TO THE MAUTHAUSEN CONCENTRATION CAMP.

AFTER A SHORT TIME, MANY FAMILIES WERE NOTIFIED THAT THEIR HUSBANDS, FATHERS, AND SONS "HAD DIED"...

SNAPSHOT: CONCENTRATION CAMPS

THE FIRST NAZI CONCENTRATION CAMP WAS ESTABLISHED IN DACHAU, ABOUT TEN MILES NORTHWEST OF MUNICH, ON MARCH 22, 1933, TO HOLD GERMANS WHO WERE OPPOSING HITLER AND HIS REGIME AND GROUPS THAT DID NOT FIT THE NAZI IDEOLOGY.

PRISONERS WERE IDENTIFIED BY COLORED TRIANGLES ON THEIR UNIFORMS. POLITICAL PRISONERS WORE RED PATCHES; CRIMINALS, GREEN; "ASOCIALS," BLACK; HOMOSEXUALS, PINK; JEHOVAH'S WITNESSES, PURPLE; EMIGRANTS, BLUE; AND JEWS, YELLOW.

CONDITIONS WERE APPALLING, AND TREATMENT OF PRISONERS WAS BRUTAL.

AFTER 1938--ESPECIALLY AFTER KRISTALLNACHT--MORE AND MORE JEWS IN AUSTRIA AND GERMANY WERE ARRESTED. INCREASINGLY, PRISONERS WERE USED AS A LABOR FORCE.

THE NUMBER OF CAMPS GREW WITH THE NUMBER OF PRISONERS: SACHSENHAUSEN, 1936; BUCHENWALD, 1937; FLOSSENBÜRG AND MAUTHAUSEN (AUSTRIA), 1938; RAVENSBRÜCK, 1939.

DURING THE FIRST YEARS OF THE WAR, MOBILE KILLING SQUADS CALLED EINSATZGRUPPEN WERE USED TO KILL MAINLY EASTERN EUROPEAN JEWS WITHIN NAZI-CONTROLLED TERRITORY.

STARTING IN 1941 IN OCCUPIED POLAND, EXTERMINATION CAMPS WERE ESTABLISHED: CHELMNO, BELZEC, SOBIBOR, TREBLINKA, AUSCHWITZ-BIRKENAU, AND MAJDANEK. THE FIRST EXPERIMENTS IN KILLING CAMP PRISONERS IN A GAS CHAMBER TOOK PLACE IN AUSCHWITZ IN THE AUTUMN OF 1941.

SEVERAL ACQUAINTANCES OF OURS WERE AMONG THOSE ARRESTED.

THE FRANKS AND THEIR FRIENDS WERE PAINED AND FRIGHTENED BY THE EVENTS OF FEBRUARY 1941...

MINE, TOO. THREE OF THEM, I KNOW, ARE NOW DEAD.

NOT DEAD... KILLED.

TO PROTEST THE ROUNDUP, A STRIKE WAS ORGANIZED IN AMSTERDAM AND OTHER CITIES. THOUSANDS OF PEOPLE STOPPED WORKING. BUT GERMAN FORCES QUICKLY AND VIOLENTLY SUPPRESSED IT.

INCREASINGLY AFRAID FOR HIS FAMILY'S SAFETY, OTTO REACHED OUT IN APRIL 1941 TO HIS OLD COLLEGE FRIEND NATHAN STRAUS JR., AND TO EDITH'S BROTHERS, JULIUS AND WALTER HOLLÄNDER.

IF THEY CAN'T HELP US GET INTO THE UNITED STATES, WHO CAN?

ON JUNE 22, 1941, NAZI GERMANY LAUNCHED OPERATION BARBAROSSA, THE INVASION OF THE SOVIET UNION, UTILIZING AN ARMY OF MORE THAN 3 MILLION MEN. VAST NEW TERRITORIES QUICKLY FELL UNDER GERMAN CONTROL...

...AND A MILLION JEWISH MEN, WOMEN, AND CHILDREN WERE SHOT BY THE EINSATZGRUPPEN.

WITH THEIR HELP, OTTO EXPLORED IMMIGRATING TO THE U.S. VIA CUBA, BUT...

IT IS IMPOSSIBLE TO GET FIVE EXIT PERMITS...

OH, HOW I WISH WE COULD GO TO THE SWIMMING POOL...

ANNE AND MARGOT WERE NOT AWARE OF THEIR PARENTS' WORRIES.

HOW ARE WE GOING TO STAY COOL?

54

A HAPPY EVENT OCCURRED ON JULY 16: MIEP AND JAN GIES WERE MARRIED. GUESTS WERE INVITED THE NEXT DAY TO A SPECIAL WEDDING RECEPTION HOSTED BY OTTO FRANK.

IT'S A PITY THAT MARGOT AND GRANDMA ARE SICK AND MOTHER HAD TO STAY HOME WITH THEM.

ANNE PRESENTED A SILVER TRAY, THE GIFT FROM THE FRANKS AND THE OFFICE STAFF...

...AND SERVED FOOD AND DRINKS.

YES! I AM GETTING BETTER AT THIS...

DAYS AFTER THE WEDDING, ANNE TRAVELED WITH SANNE AND HER PARENTS TO BEEKBERGEN, SOME 50 MILES OUTSIDE OF AMSTERDAM, WHERE SANNE'S AUNT AND UNCLE HAD RENTED A SUMMER HOME.

BUT THEN IT BEGAN TO RAIN AND RAIN...

SHE WROTE, "I READ A LOT, IT'S A PITY WE CAN'T GO OUT. WE SLEEP MUCH MORE PEACEFULLY HERE..."

AT LEAST THERE'S NOTHING AT ALL TO DISTURB US.

IN THE COUNTRY THERE WERE NO CONSTANT AIR-RAID ALARMS.

AND STILL IT RAINED. SHE WROTE HER FATHER: "WOULDN'T YOU BE ABLE TO COME AND VISIT ME SOMETIME? I'D ENJOY THAT SO MUCH."

BUT, DEAREST, YOU'RE FAR TOO BUSY...

PERHAPS TO MAKE UP FOR NOT HAVING BEEN ABLE TO VISIT ANNE IN BEEKBERGEN, OTTO TOOK HER TO A COUNTRY HOTEL NEAR ARNHEM, CALLED THE GROOT WARNSBORN, FOR SEVERAL DAYS IN SEPTEMBER 1941.

PIM, THE HOTEL IS SO-O-O-O BEAUTIFUL!

YES. AND IT IS SO QUIET.

AFTER OTTO AND ANNE RETURNED, AMSTERDAM BECAME COVERED WITH SIGNS FORBIDDING JEWS TO ENTER VARIOUS PUBLIC PLACES.

THEY'RE ALL OVER, PIM.

CINEAC

Voor Joden verboden

Voor Joden verboden

Voor Joden verboden

Voor Joden verboden

Voor Joden verboden

Voor Joden verboden

Voor Joden verboden

Voor ve

NO MATTER. WE'LL JUST PLAY MOVIES AT HOME...

THEY TRIED TO FIND WAYS TO COPE WITH ALL THE ANTI-JEWISH MEASURES.

AT THIS TIME, ANNE AND MARGOT STARTED TO FOLLOW CLASSES IN JUDAISM AT THE HOME OF RABBI MEHLER...

...AND MARGOT ALSO BECAME A MEMBER OF A ZIONIST YOUTH GROUP.

58

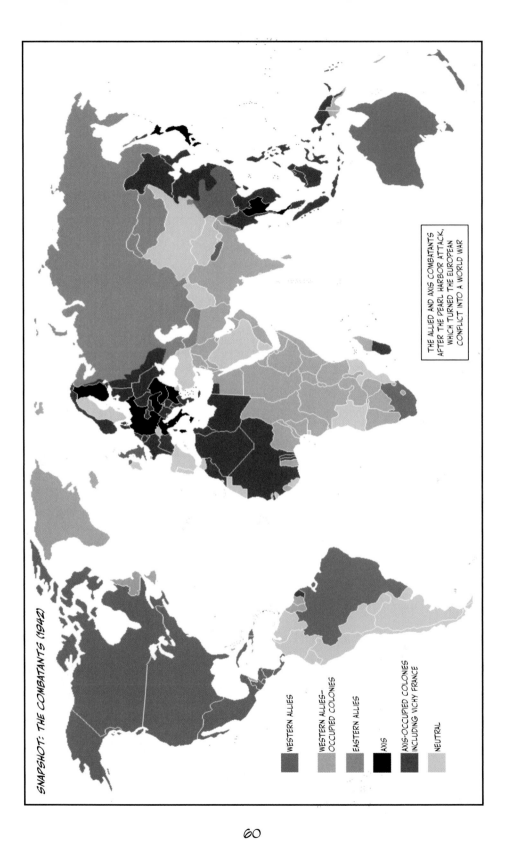

SNAPSHOT: THE COMBATANTS (1942)

THE ALLIED AND AXIS COMBATANTS
AFTER THE PEARL HARBOR ATTACK,
WHICH TURNED THE EUROPEAN
CONFLICT INTO A WORLD WAR

WESTERN ALLIES

WESTERN ALLIES-
OCCUPIED COLONIES

EASTERN ALLIES

AXIS

AXIS-OCCUPIED COLONIES
INCLUDING VICHY FRANCE

NEUTRAL

SNAPSHOT: THE WANNSEE CONFERENCE

HITLER AND THE NAZIS REGARDED THE JEWS AS THEIR GREATEST ENEMY. IN THE SECOND HALF OF 1941, HITLER HAD DECIDED TO KILL ALL THE JEWS OF EUROPE. A SECRET MEETING TO DISCUSS THIS WAS PLANNED, BUT HAD TO BE POSTPONED BECAUSE OF PEARL HARBOR. ON JANUARY 20, 1942, THE MEETING OF 15 HIGH-RANKING CIVIL SERVANTS AND SS OFFICERS WAS HELD IN A VILLA NEAR THE WANNSEE LAKE IN BERLIN. THE MEETING PLANNED THE "FINAL SOLUTION" TO THE SO-CALLED JEWISH QUESTION. THIS "WANNSEE CONFERENCE," CONVENED AND LED BY REINHARD HEYDRICH, THEN CHIEF OF THE NAZI SECURITY POLICE AND SECRET SERVICE, LASTED ABOUT AN HOUR AND A HALF.

ADOLF EICHMANN, A GESTAPO HEAD AND ONE OF THE ATTENDEES, HAD DRAFTED A LIST OF THE NUMBER OF JEWS IN VARIOUS EUROPEAN COUNTRIES THAT THEY EXPECTED TO DEAL WITH. THERE WAS A TOTAL OF 11 MILLION, WITH THE LARGEST NUMBERS IN THE U.S.S.R., POLAND, AND HUNGARY.

Protektorat Böhmen und Mähren		74.200
Estland — judenfrei —		
Lettland		3.500
Litauen		34.000
Belgien		43.000
Dänemark		5.600
Frankreich / Besetztes Gebiet		165.000
Unbesetztes Gebiet		700.000
Griechenland		69.600
Niederlande		160.800
Norwegen		1.300
B. Bulgarien		48.000
England		330.000
Finnland		2.300
Irland		4.000
Italien einschl. Sardinien		58.000
Albanien		200
Kroatien		40.000
Portugal		3.000
Rumänien einschl. Bessarabien		342.000
Schweden		8.000
Schweiz		18.000
Serbien		10.000
Slowakei		88.000
Spanien		6.000
Türkei (europ. Teil)		55.500
Ungarn		742.800
UdSSR		5.000.000
Ukraine	2.994.684	
Weißrußland aus- schl. Bialystok	446.484	
Zusammen:	über	11.000.000

K210405   372829

HEYDRICH OPENED THE MEETING WITH THE ANNOUNCEMENT THAT REICH MARSHAL HERMANN GÖRING HAD PUT HIM IN CHARGE OF PREPARATIONS FOR THE FINAL SOLUTION TO THE JEWISH QUESTION.
HE DECLARED: "UNDER PROPER GUIDANCE, IN THE COURSE OF THE FINAL SOLUTION, THE JEWS ARE TO BE ALLOCATED FOR APPROPRIATE LABOR IN THE EAST..."
"...IN THE COURSE OF WHICH ACTION DOUBTLESS A LARGE PORTION WILL BE ELIMINATED BY NATURAL CAUSES."
HE THEN ADDED: "THE POSSIBLE FINAL REMNANT WILL...HAVE TO BE TREATED ACCORDINGLY BECAUSE IT...WOULD, IF RELEASED, ACT AS THE SEED OF A NEW JEWISH REVIVAL."

SPEAKING ABOUT THE CONFERENCE IN 1960, ADOLF EICHMANN SAID: "I REMEMBER AT THE END OF THIS WANNSEE CONFERENCE, HEYDRICH, MÜLLER, AND MYSELF SETTLED DOWN COMFORTABLY BY THE FIREPLACE..."

THERE WAS NO DOUBT THAT THE WORDS "ELIMINATED BY NATURAL CAUSES" AND "TREATED ACCORDINGLY" CONVICTED ALL EUROPEAN JEWS TO DEATH.

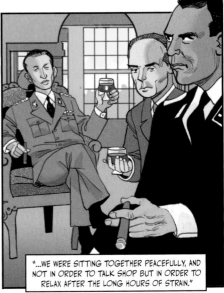

"...WE WERE SITTING TOGETHER PEACEFULLY, AND NOT IN ORDER TO TALK SHOP BUT IN ORDER TO RELAX AFTER THE LONG HOURS OF STRAIN."

THE NEW YEAR OF 1942 BEGAN SADLY FOR THE FRANKS. GRANDMA HOLLÄNDER DIED FROM CANCER ON JANUARY 29 AND WAS BURIED IN A JEWISH CEMETERY OUTSIDE AMSTERDAM.

AND RUMORS THAT JEWS WOULD HAVE TO GO TO WORK CAMPS BECAME STRONGER.

HERMANN, WE NEED TO BE PREPARED. THE ANNEX WOULD BE A GOOD HIDING PLACE...

...AND LARGE ENOUGH FOR SEVEN PEOPLE. WE NEED TO DISCUSS IT WITH KUGLER AND KLEIMAN.

JOHANNES KLEIMAN AND VICTOR KUGLER AGREED TO HELP. DURING THE FOLLOWING WEEKS, SECRETLY AND AFTER HOURS, JOHANNES KLEIMAN AND HIS BROTHER BROUGHT FURNITURE AND FOOD TO THE ANNEX.

IN LATE APRIL, THE NAZIS DECREED THAT ALL JEWS OVER SIX YEARS OF AGE IN THE NETHERLANDS WERE TO BE IDENTIFIED BY THE JEWISH STAR.

REMEMBER, ANNE, IT HAS TO BE VISIBLE AT ALL TIMES...

YES, MUMMY...

THE NETHERLANDS WAS NOT THE ONLY COUNTRY RULED BY THE NAZIS WHERE JEWS HAD TO WEAR A STAR.

WHEN HIS EMPLOYEES SAW OTTO ARRIVING IN THE OFFICE BEARING HIS STAR, THEY JUST PRETENDED IT WASN'T THERE.

GOOD MORNING, OTTO.

GOOD MORNING, MR. FRANK.

62

63

CHAPTER 6

The Diary

65

ANNE'S BIRTHDAY PARTY, HELD TWO DAYS LATER, WAS A HUGE SUCCESS. SHE INVITED HER ENTIRE CLASS FROM THE JEWISH LYCEUM. THE CAKE EDITH MADE WAS DELICIOUS.

AS GOING TO MOVIES WAS FORBIDDEN, A RIN TIN TIN MOVIE, ONE OF ANNE'S FAVORITES, WAS SHOWN.

RIN TIN TIN

A JUNE 30, 1942, DECREE ORDERED JEWS IN THE NETHERLANDS TO KEEP AN EVENING CURFEW OF 8 O'CLOCK AND FORBADE THEM TO USE PUBLIC TRANSPORTATION. IN AMSTERDAM, JEWS WERE STILL ALLOWED TO CYCLE.

SOON AFTER THE BIRTHDAY CELEBRATION, ANNE AND MARGOT RETURNED TO STUDYING.

YES, FINALLY...

THANK GOODNESS, THE HOLIDAYS ARE NEARLY HERE!

BY THEN, ANNE HAD DEVELOPED NEW INTERESTS. READING WAS ONE SHE SHARED...

I LOVE THE JOOP TER HEUL BOOKS BY CISSY VAN MARXVELDT!

THIS ONE IS WONDERFUL.

...WITH HER FRIEND JACQUELINE VAN MAARSEN.

ANNE AND JACQUELINE ALSO ORGANIZED SPECIAL MOVIE MATINEES. THEY EVEN MADE OFFICIAL TICKETS.

HOW MANY DO WE HAVE?

WE'RE ALMOST DONE!

BOYS AND GIRLS THEY FAVORED WERE INVITED.

TICKETS, PLEASE.

YOU'RE IN ROW 5, SEAT 2.

BUT THE BOY MOST ON ANNE'S MIND NEVER CAME...

PETER SCHIFF! TWO SUMMERS AGO I HAD SUCH A CRUSH ON HIM...

BUT THE 15-YEAR-OLD GERMAN ÉMIGRÉ'S INTEREST IN ANNE HADN'T LASTED.

NOW HE THINKS I AM TOO YOUNG.

HE DOESN'T EVEN NOTICE ME ANYMORE.

BUT SOMEONE ELSE NOTICED HER.

I THINK HE'S LOOKING AT ME.

ANNE'S PARENTS HAD OTHER WORRIES. AS THERE WERE RUMORS THAT JEWS WOULD HAVE TO GO TO WORK CAMPS, THEY PLANNED TO GO INTO HIDING ON JULY 16. BUT ON SUNDAY, JULY 5...

MARGOT FRANK-- I HAVE A CARD FOR MARGOT FRANK...

OH, GOD! A CALL-UP!

EDITH WENT TO GET HERMANN VAN PELS, BUT FIRST TOLD MARGOT TO TELL HER SISTER...

ANNE, DADDY HAS BEEN CALLED UP. HE MUST REPORT TO THE SS.

OH, NO!

DON'T WORRY, HE'S NOT GOING. MUMMY AND DADDY HAVE TAKEN PRECAUTIONS.

RETURNING WITH HERMANN, EDITH SAID...

GIRLS, PLEASE GO TO YOUR ROOM. I NEED TO TALK TO MR. VAN PELS

WHEN IS OTTO DUE HOME?

AT 5 O'CLOCK, OTTO FINALLY RETURNED FROM VISITING AN ACQUAINTANCE...

WE MUST GO TOMORROW EVEN THOUGH THE HIDING PLACE IS NOT READY...I'VE GOT TO SPEAK TO JO NOW. WHERE ARE THE GIRLS?

THEY ARE IN THEIR ROOM, PACKING.

MARGOT AND ANNE STARTED TO PACK...

HIDE, WHERE ARE WE GOING TO HIDE?

IN THE CITY? IN THE COUNTRY? IN A SHACK?

ANNE, IT'S NOT DADDY... I HAVE TO REPORT TO THE SS... BUT WE ARE GOING TO HIDE...

AND THE DIARY WAS OF COURSE THE FIRST THING ANNE PACKED.

THE ENTIRE ANNEX WAS LESS THAN 700 SQUARE FEET (SEE ROOM DIMENSIONS BELOW). THIS WAS TO BE THE LIVING SPACE FOR THE FOUR FRANK FAMILY MEMBERS AS WELL AS FOR HERMANN AND AUGUSTE VAN PELS AND THEIR SON, PETER.

MEASUREMENTS OF THE SECRET ANNEX

ANNE AND MARGOT'S ROOM
16.57 FT X 6.86 FT, HEIGHT 9.28 FT

OTTO AND EDITH'S ROOM
16.50 FT X 10.27 FT, HEIGHT 9.28 FT

COMMON LIVING ROOM AND HERMANN AND AUGUST VAN PELS'S BEDROOM
18.64 FT X 16.86 FT, HEIGHT 8.63 FT

PETER VAN PELS'S ROOM
12.83 FT X 6.92 FT, HEIGHT 8.63 FT

ATTIC
23.95 FT X 18.64 FT

EDITH AND MARGOT WERE TOO TENSE TO WORK. BUT OTTO AND ANNE BEGAN RIGHT AWAY, UNPACKING, STOCKING CABINETS, AND ADJUSTING FURNITURE.

IT TOOK THE FOUR OF THEM TWO FULL DAYS TO ACCOMPLISH THIS FEAT.

ONLY THEN DID ANNE FIND THE TIME TO WRITE IN HER DIARY AGAIN...

IT SEEMS LIKE YEARS SINCE SUNDAY MORNING. SO MUCH HAS HAPPENED, IT'S AS IF THE WHOLE WORLD HAS SUDDENLY TURNED UPSIDE DOWN.

ANNE DESCRIBED THE BUILDING IN DETAIL. OTTO AND EDITH SLEPT IN ONE ROOM.

ANNE AND MARGOT SHARED A SMALLER ROOM.

THE KITCHEN AND LIVING-DINING ROOM ON THE THIRD FLOOR BECAME A BEDROOM FOR THE VAN PELSES AT NIGHT.

PETER VAN PELS HAD A SMALL ROOM TO HIMSELF.

THE ATTIC LOOKED MUCH LIKE THIS...

AND THE WASHROOM WAS USED BY EVERYONE.

ONE IMMEDIATE JOY FOR ANNE WAS THAT HER FATHER HAD REMEMBERED TO BRING HER COLLECTION OF MOVIE STAR PHOTOS AND POSTCARDS, MANY OF WHICH SHE HAPPILY GLUED ON THE WALLS.

THAT'S MUCH MORE CHEERFUL.

DEANNA DURBIN, SONJA HENIE, NORMA SHEARER, GINGER ROGERS, RAY MILLAND, AND MANY OTHER STARS OF THE MOMENT SMILED DOWN AT HER EACH DAY.

ANNE CAME TO APPRECIATE THAT THEY WERE COMPLETELY DEPENDENT ON THEIR HELPERS. SHE DID NOT REALIZE THIS AT THE BEGINNING, BUT ON JANUARY 28, 1944, SHE WROTE:

"NEVER HAVE THEY UTTERED A SINGLE WORD ABOUT THE BURDEN WE MUST BE... THEY COME UPSTAIRS EVERY DAY AND TALK...PUT ON THEIR MOST CHEERFUL EXPRESSIONS...AND ARE ALWAYS READY TO DO WHAT THEY CAN. WHILE OTHERS DISPLAY THEIR HEROISM IN BATTLE OR AGAINST THE GERMANS, OUR HELPERS PROVE THEIRS EVERY DAY BY THEIR GOOD SPIRITS AND AFFECTION."

JOHANNES KLEIMAN

MIEP GIES

VICTOR KUGLER

BEP VOSKUIJL

JAN GIES

75

76

78

"WE LIVE IN A PARADISE COMPARED TO THE JEWS WHO AREN'T IN HIDING."

...THE SPOT ON WHICH WE'RE STANDING IS STILL SAFE, BUT THE CLOUDS ARE MOVING IN ON US.

SNAPSHOT: THE OTHER JEWS

THERE WERE APPROXIMATELY 140,000 JEWS LIVING IN THE NETHERLANDS IN 1940.

SEVENTY-FIVE PERCENT OF THEM WERE DEPORTED TO THE CONCENTRATION-- AND EXTERMINATION-- CAMPS. IN TOTAL, 102,000 JEWISH MEN, WOMEN, AND CHILDREN WERE KILLED.

MANY JEWS IN HIDING FACED MORE DIFFICULT AND TRAGIC TIMES THAN THOSE AT 263 PRINSENGRACHT. FINDING A HIDING PLACE WAS DIFFICULT. OFTEN FAMILY MEMBERS HAD TO BE SEPARATED FROM EACH OTHER AS HIDING PLACES WERE TOO SMALL, THE RISK WAS CONSIDERED TOO GREAT, OR IT WAS FINANCIALLY IMPOSSIBLE.

SOMETIMES THEY HAD TO KEEP MOVING FROM ONE ADDRESS TO ANOTHER.

IT'S ESTIMATED THAT SOME 28,000 JEWS MANAGED TO GO INTO HIDING, SOME 19,000 SURVIVED, AND 9,000 WERE ARRESTED AND DEPORTED. THOSE ARRESTED WERE OFTEN BETRAYED. THERE WAS EVEN A SPECIAL UNIT, CONSISTING OF AROUND 50 DUTCH NAZIS AND KNOWN AS THE HENNEICKE COLUMN, WHICH CAPTURED JEWS IN HIDING AND DELIVERED THEM TO THEIR NAZI OCCUPIERS FOR A SUM OF MONEY.

JEWS ARE REGULARLY KILLED BY MACHINE-GUN FIRE, HAND GRENADES, AND EVEN POISONED BY GAS.

NEWS FROM THE OUTSIDE WORLD QUICKLY WENT FROM BAD TO WORSE...ON OCTOBER 9, ANNE WROTE: "OUR MANY JEWISH FRIENDS AND ACQUAINTANCES ARE BEING TAKEN AWAY IN DROVES" AND TRANSPORTED "IN CATTLE CARS TO WESTERBORK."

"TONIGHT I DREAMED ABOUT PETER SCHIFF..."

"I WISH HE WOULD COME AND HIDE WITH US. PERHAPS THE POOR BOY IS ALREADY DEAD IN POLAND."

DESPITE ALL THE FEAR AND BAD NEWS, ANNE AND MARGOT STILL TALKED ABOUT THE FUTURE.

I WANT TO BECOME A MATERNITY NURSE IN PALESTINE.

THAT'S A NICE PROFESSION. BUT I'D PREFER TO WORK WITH TODDLERS.

AND THE NEWS WAS NOT ALL BAD...

IN EARLY NOVEMBER, ANNE MADE NOTE OF ALLIED VICTORIES IN AFRICA AND OF THE SOVIET ARMIES HOLDING AGAINST NAZI FORCES IN STALINGRAD.

WE'LL HAVE COFFEE AND TEA TO CELEBRATE!

FINALLY SOME GOOD NEWS...

ON NOVEMBER 9, ANNE DESCRIBED HOW THE ANNEX GOT MUCH OF ITS FOOD.

...AND JUST RECENTLY 300 POUNDS OF BEANS HAD BEEN PURCHASED TO BE SHARED BETWEEN THEM AND THE HELPERS.

BREAD WAS DELIVERED DAILY BY A BAKER, "A FRIEND OF MR. KLEIMAN'S," RATION BOOKS HAD BEEN BOUGHT ON THE BLACK MARKET, "HUNDREDS OF CANS OF FOOD" HAD BEEN PREVIOUSLY STORED...

SHORTLY AFTER THE FAMILIES HAD GONE INTO HIDING, JOHAN VOSKUIJL (BEP'S FATHER), WHO WORKED IN THE WAREHOUSE, BUILT A MOVABLE BOOKCASE TO STAND IN FRONT OF AND CAMOUFLAGE THE ENTRY DOOR TO THE SECRET ANNEX.

AS CONDITIONS FOR JEWS WORSENED, AND WITH THE ANNEX NOW STOCKED WITH FOOD AND CAMOUFLAGED BY THE BOOKCASE, ANNE ANNOUNCED ON NOVEMBER 10, "WE'RE PLANNING TO TAKE AN EIGHTH PERSON INTO HIDING WITH US!"

IT'S JUST AS DANGEROUS, WHETHER THERE ARE SEVEN OR EIGHT.

THEY CHOSE THEIR FRIEND FRITZ PFEFFER, A DENTIST.

FIRST, HOWEVER, OTTO FELT HE HAD TO SPEAK WITH KUGLER AND KLEIMAN, WHO BRAVELY ANSWERED...

"WE'LL ASK HIM TO BRING ALONG SOMETHING TO FILL OUR CAVITIES WITH," ANNE WROTE.

CHAPTER 7

The Eight Hiders

FRITZ PFEFFER WAS INSTRUCTED BY MIEP GIES TO WALK BACK AND FORTH IN FRONT OF THE MAIN POST OFFICE AT 11 A.M. ON NOVEMBER 16, AND "A MAN WOULD MEET HIM THERE."

JOHANNES KLEIMAN SOON APPEARED AND, ACCORDING TO ANNE'S DIARY, TOLD PFEFFER THAT THE MAN HE WAS EXPECTING COULDN'T COME AND THAT HE SHOULD...

DROP BY THE OFFICE TO SEE MIEP.

KLEIMAN TOOK THE STREETCAR TO GET TO THE OFFICE, WHILE PFEFFER, BEING JEWISH, HAD TO WALK.

FRITZ ARRIVED AT ABOUT 11:20, AND MIEP TOOK HIM UP THE STEEP STAIRWAY TO THE BOOKCASE DOOR.

I EXPECTED TO HIDE SOMEWHERE IN THE COUNTRY, NOT HERE IN THE MIDDLE OF THE CITY.

YOU WON'T BE SORRY, I PROMISE.

MOMENTS LATER, MIEP TOOK HIM UP ANOTHER FLIGHT OF STAIRS TO THE VAN PELSES' ROOM. THE FAMILIES WERE WAITING WITH COFFEE, COGNAC, AND HUGE SMILES.

OTTO? I THOUGHT YOU WERE IN BELGIUM!

NO, BUT I'M GLAD THE WORLD WE LEFT BEHIND BELIEVES SO.

SIT DOWN, FRITZ, MAKE YOURSELF AT HOME. HAVE A DRINK.

86

STILL IN TOTAL SURPRISE, PFEFFER SLOWLY ABSORBED THE STORY OF THE FRANKS' AND VAN PELSES' ESCAPE TO THIS HIDEAWAY.

YOU AND ANNE WILL SHARE HER ROOM, AND MARGOT WILL MOVE IN WITH US.

I WILL APPRECIATE WHEREVER YOU PUT ME.

AFTER A MUCH-NEEDED NAP, PFEFFER PUT AWAY HIS THINGS, WHICH MIEP HAD PREVIOUSLY BROUGHT TO THE ANNEX...

...AND THEN LAUGHED AT HERMANN VAN PELS'S IRONIC SET OF RULES.

A UNIQUE FACILITY FOR THE TEMPORARY ACCOMMODATION OF JEWS AND OTHER DISPOSSESSED PERSONS...

"OPEN ALL YEAR ROUND, LOCATED IN BEAUTIFUL, QUIET WOODED SURROUNDINGS IN THE HEART OF AMSTERDAM."

ANNE'S FIRST APPRAISAL OF PFEFFER WAS THAT HE WAS...

A VERY NICE MAN, DADDY.

I'M GLAD TO MAKE THE SMALL SACRIFICE OF SHARING MY ROOM WITH HIM.

BUT PFEFFER ALSO BROUGHT SOME TRAGIC NEWS TO THE ANNEX.

SO MANY OF OUR FRIENDS HAVE BEEN TAKEN TO A DREADFUL FATE.

EVERY NIGHT MILITARY VEHICLES CRUISE THE STREETS LOOKING FOR JEWS.

AND THEY'RE OFFERING CITIZENS BOUNTIES FOR BETRAYING HIDDEN JEWS.

88

AS WEEKS TURNED INTO MONTHS, ANNE AND HER MOTHER CLASHED AGAIN AND AGAIN.

I DON'T CARE WHAT YOU SAY. WHY DON'T YOU JUST WASH YOUR HANDS OF ME?

ANNE!

"I WISH I COULD ASK GOD TO GIVE ME ANOTHER PERSONALITY," SHE SADLY CONFESSED.

THE GERMAN 6TH ARMY SURRENDERED TO SOVIET FORCES IN STALINGRAD ON FEBRUARY 2, THE FIRST TURNING POINT IN THE WAR.

IN MARCH 1943, RADIO NEWS INCLUDED WOUNDED GERMAN SOLDIERS REPORTING TO HITLER.

"LIEUTENANT NIEDECK. WOUNDED IN DECEMBER '41, WEST OF MOSCOW. SHRAPNEL IN MY RIGHT UPPER AND LOWER ARM AND FROSTBITTEN FEET."

"HOW ARE YOUR FEET? BETTER?"

"THE WOUND ON MY RIGHT FOOT IS STILL OPEN. I CAN'T WALK YET."

WHAT A HIDEOUS PUPPET SHOW...

IN MARCH, ANNE WROTE, "I STILL HAVEN'T GOT OVER MY FEARS OF PLANES AND SHOOTING."

LET ME TELL YOU A STORY...

SHE OFTEN CRAWLED INTO HER FATHER'S BED FOR COMFORT.

TOWARD THE END OF MARCH, THE PAPERS QUOTED A HATEFUL SPEECH BY HANNS ALBIN RAUTER, THE LEADER OF THE SS AND POLICE IN THE NETHERLANDS...

LISTEN TO THIS: RAUTER WANTS TO GET RID OF 130,000 JEWS.

SHIPPED OFF TO FILTHY SLAUGHTERHOUSES...

92

93

HER MOTHER BOTH HAD A GOOD APPETITE AND ENJOYED TALKING.

I WON'T LISTEN TO ANYTHING YOU SAY ABOUT MARGOT.

OTTO WAS THE "MOST MODEST PERSON AT THE TABLE."

NO, NO, I HAVE HAD ENOUGH.

BUT ANNE ACCUSED FRITZ PFEFFER OF DEVOURING GREAT PORTIONS AND SPEAKING ONLY OF...

...FOOD! THIS IS MADE SO WELL!

ON SEPTEMBER 8, THE 7 O'CLOCK NEWS ANNOUNCED...

"ITALY HAS SURRENDERED TO THE ALLIES!"

ON SEPTEMBER 16, ANNE WROTE OF HER FEARS OF THE "UNRELIABLE" AND TOO CURIOUS WILLEM VAN MAAREN, WHO HAD REPLACED BEP'S ILL FATHER IN THE WAREHOUSE.

I'M GOING TO LOOK AT THE RECORDS.

SOMETHING STRANGE IS GOING ON HERE...

95

IN OCTOBER, ANNE CONTINUED TO WRITE ABOUT THE ANTAGONISMS IN THE ANNEX AS WELL AS MARGOT'S HEADACHES,

MR. PFEFFER'S SLEEPLESSNESS,

MRS. VAN PELS'S MOODS,

AND HER OWN DEPRESSION.

ANNE STATED THAT SHE DIDN'T "GIVE A DASH" ABOUT HER MOTHER AND MARGOT...

...AND THAT THERE WAS NO ONE SHE LOVED MORE THAN HER FATHER.

AS FAR AS I'M CONCERNED, THEY CAN GO JUMP IN THE LAKE!

ON OCTOBER 2, 1943, AND ACTING ON A NAZI ATTEMPT TO DEPORT JEWS, THE DANISH UNDERGROUND HEROICALLY SMUGGLED 7,200 JEWS TO THE COAST, WHERE DANISH FISHERMEN FERRIED THEM TO SWEDEN, WHICH HAD OFFERED ASYLUM.

AROUND 500 JEWS WERE CAPTURED AND DEPORTED TO CONCENTRATION CAMPS BY THE GERMANS.

ON NOVEMBER 3-4, THE NAZIS KILLED 43,000 JEWS IN A PLANNED MASSACRE IN THREE CONCENTRATION CAMPS IN POLAND.

IN LATE 1943, ANNE FELT COMPLETELY ISOLATED AND LONGED...

...TO RIDE A BIKE, DANCE, WHISTLE, LOOK AT THE WORLD, FEEL YOUNG, AND KNOW THAT I'M FREE.

YET SHE COULDN'T LET IT SHOW. "JUST IMAGINE WHAT WOULD HAPPEN IF ALL EIGHT OF US WERE TO FEEL SORRY FOR OURSELVES."

FROM NOVEMBER 28 TO DECEMBER 1, CHURCHILL, ROOSEVELT, AND STALIN MET IN TEHRAN, IRAN, TO DISCUSS THE INVASION OF GERMANY FROM THE WEST.

97

CHAPTER 8

The New Year

IN EARLY JANUARY 1944, ANNE REVEALED A CHANGE OF HEART TOWARD HER MOTHER.

IT'S TRUE SHE DIDN'T UNDERSTAND ME...

BUT I DIDN'T UNDERSTAND HER, EITHER.

WHILE ANNE COULDN'T LOVE EDITH "WITH THE DEVOTION OF A CHILD," SHE REALIZED THINGS BETWEEN THEM WERE BETTER.

SHE ALSO REALIZED THAT MANY FIGHTS WERE DUE TO THEIR BEING IN HIDING AND UNABLE TO GO OUTSIDE.

ANNE WAS ENTERING PUBERTY AND LOVED THE "WONDROUS" CHANGES IT BROUGHT...

...THE JOY OF HER PERIODS AND THE WARM FEELING OF "CARRYING AROUND A SWEET SECRET."

I'VE BECOME AN INDEPENDENT PERSON SOONER THAN MOST GIRLS.

IN NEED OF SOMEONE TO TALK TO, SHE FOUND A PRETEXT TO TALK TO PETER VAN PELS...

CAN I HELP YOU WITH THAT CROSSWORD PUZZLE?

YES...

AT MUCH THE SAME TIME, SHE DREAMED OF ANOTHER PETER, PETER SCHIFF... AND WAS SURE THAT THIS PETER WAS THE ONLY ONE FOR HER.

IF I HAD ONLY KNOWN, I WOULD HAVE COME TO YOU LONG AGO!

SHE REMINISCED ABOUT THEIR WALKING HAND IN HAND THROUGH THEIR NEIGHBORHOOD...

...AND IMAGINED THEM TOGETHER IN THE ANNEX.

OH, PETER.

SHE FELT THAT SHE LOVED HIM WITH ALL HER HEART.

IN EARLY FEBRUARY, NEWSPAPERS WERE FILLED WITH STORIES ABOUT A POSSIBLE ALLIED INVASION OF THE NETHERLANDS AND ABOUT GERMAN PLANS TO FLOOD AMSTERDAM AND OTHER AREAS TO STOP AN ALLIED ADVANCE.

ANNE DECIDED TO "CONCENTRATE ON STUDYING" AND KEEP UP HER WRITING.

SHE OBSERVED THE WAY HER FATHER KISSED HER MOTHER...

HE KISSES HER LIKE HE KISSES MARGOT AND ME.

...AND DECIDED THAT HE DID NOT LOVE EDITH, AT LEAST NOT THE WAY THAT SHE DESIRED A HUSBAND TO LOVE HER!

SHE BEGAN TO NOTICE THE WAY PETER CONSTANTLY LOOKED AT HER...

PETER, AFTER AN ARGUMENT WITH MR. PFEFFER, SOUGHT OUT ANNE IN THE ATTIC.

I DON'T USUALLY TALK MUCH BECAUSE I GET TONGUE-TIED.

YOU'RE NEVER AT A LOSS FOR WORDS. YOU SAY EXACTLY WHAT YOU WANT TO SAY.

YOU'RE WRONG. I TALK TOO MUCH AND THAT'S JUST AS BAD.

"I SENSED A STRONG FEELING OF FELLOWSHIP," ANNE WROTE LATER, SUCH AS SHE HAD ONLY EVER ENJOYED WITH GIRLFRIENDS.

IN THE FOLLOWING DAYS, ANNE VISITED PETER MORE AND MORE.

WHAT ARE YOU DOING?

I'M STUDYING FRENCH.

SHALL I HELP YOU?

ANY REASON BROUGHT HER UP TO THE ATTIC...THROUGH PETER'S ROOM.

I NEED SOME POTATOES FROM THE ATTIC.

I'LL GO!

"IT'S ALWAYS SO I CAN SEE HIM," ANNE WROTE ON FEBRUARY 18.

ON FEBRUARY 20, ANNE DESCRIBED A TYPICAL SUNDAY.

MR. PFEFFER WOULD RISE AT 8 O'CLOCK, SPEND AN HOUR CLEANING HIMSELF, THEN PRAY FOR FIFTEEN MINUTES WHILE MRS. VAN PELS USED THE BATHROOM.

BY 9:30 THE BLACKOUT SCREENS WERE REMOVED. THEN, WHEN OTHER PEOPLE MIGHT STROLL IN THE SUN, THEY BATHED AND CLEANED, KNOWING THEY WOULDN'T BE HEARD.

YOU WERE ALWAYS SURROUNDED BY A FLOCK OF GIRLS AND AT LEAST TWO BOYS...ALWAYS THE CENTER OF ATTENTION...

MOVING BEYOND CROSSWORD PUZZLES AND STUDIES, ANNE AND PETER TALKED ABOUT THEIR PASTS, THEIR PARENTS...

YES, I REMEMBER THAT...

OH, IF I THINK OF HOW I USED TO BE...

I WAS SO SUPERFICIAL.

IN THE FIRST HALF OF 1943, SHE HAD SUFFERED "CRYING SPELLS," PROFOUND "LONELINESS," AND AWARENESS OF HER OWN FAULTS.

BUT SHE HAD MATURED INTO A TEENAGER WHO "BEGAN TO THINK ABOUT THINGS AND TO WRITE STORIES."

HOW ABOUT A LITTLE BEAR DISCOVERING THE WORLD...

AND SHE DIDN'T TRUST ANYONE BUT HERSELF.

AND NOW? NOW SHE LIVED "ONLY FOR PETER," AND UNLIKE HER MOTHER...

...SHE WAS OPTIMISTIC, AS "BEAUTY REMAINS, EVEN IN MISFORTUNE."

ON MARCH 31, HOPE AND JOY FILLED THE ANNEX AFTER THE HIDERS LEARNED OF THE RUSSIAN ARMY'S RECENT VICTORIES.

THEY'VE REACHED THE POLISH BORDER!

AND THE PRUT RIVER IN ROMANIA!

THEY'RE APPROACHING ODESSA!

BUT ANNE THOUGHT ALSO OF THE JEWS IN GERMAN-OCCUPIED HUNGARY: "THEY, TOO, ARE DOOMED."

THIS IS THE TENTH TIME THIS WEEK THAT WE'VE HAD SAUERKRAUT.

IN THE ANNEX, THE RATIONS WERE MEAGER.

OH, YOU POOR GIRL...

ON APRIL 5, ANNE FORMALLY DECLARED HER NEED TO STUDY HARDER SO SHE COULD BECOME...

A JOURNALIST! THAT'S WHAT I WANT TO BE.

I KNOW I CAN WRITE.

SHE LIKED "EVA'S DREAM" AND SOME OTHER SHORT STORIES SHE HAD WRITTEN...

BUT--AND THAT'S A BIG QUESTION-- WILL I EVER WRITE SOMETHING GREAT?

I WANT TO GO ON LIVING EVEN AFTER MY DEATH. THAT'S WHY I'M SO GRATEFUL TO GOD FOR HAVING GIVEN ME THIS GIFT.

105

IN EARLY APRIL, ANNE MADE A LIST OF WHAT SHE CALLED "HOBBIES AND INTERESTS." THOSE SHE LISTED WERE...
1. WRITING (WHICH ANNE CONSIDERED MORE THAN A HOBBY)
2. GENEALOGICAL CHARTS (PARTICULARLY OF ROYAL FAMILIES)
3. HISTORY (HER FATHER HAD GIVEN HER MANY BOOKS, OUT OF WHICH SHE COPIED PASSAGES)
4. GREEK AND ROMAN MYTHOLOGY (SHE HAD MEMORIZED THE NINE MUSES, THE SEVEN LOVES OF ZEUS, THE WIVES OF HERCULES)
5. AND MOVIE STARS, FAMILY PHOTOGRAPHS, AND READING (IN FACT, ANNE MENTIONED MORE THAN 25 BOOKS BY NAME)

THE NIGHT OF APRIL 15, EASTER SUNDAY, BEGAN LIKE ANY OTHER, UNTIL...

I AM HAVING TROUBLE WITH AN ENGLISH SENTENCE. CAN YOU HELP ME?

SOUNDS FISHY...

ANNE WAS RIGHT: A BURGLARY WAS TAKING PLACE...

THE MEN INVESTIGATED WHILE THE FOUR WOMEN WAITED, WHEN SUDDENLY...

BANG!

AT TEN O'CLOCK, OTTO AND MR. VAN PELS APPEARED...

LIGHTS OUT, TIPTOE UPSTAIRS.

WE'RE EXPECTING THE POLICE.

BUT THE BURGLARS RETURNED...

SLAM!

BLAM!

...WHICH CAUSED VAN PELS TO BECOME FURIOUS, AND BRAVE...

THIS TIME THEY LEFT FOR GOOD.

BUT SOON AFTER, PASSERSBY SHONE A FLASHLIGHT THROUGH THE OPENING. THE MEN RUSHED BACK UPSTAIRS, EXPECTING THE POLICE ANY MINUTE.

THEN, AT A QUARTER PAST ELEVEN...

TAP, TAP, TAP

OH NO, THEY ARE AT THE BOOKCASE...WE ARE LOST...

TAP, TAP, TAP

BUT WAIT! THEY ARE LEAVING!

LOOKING BACK ON THAT FEARFUL NIGHT, ANNE CONCLUDED: "GOD WAS TRULY WATCHING OVER US...IF GOD LETS ME LIVE, I'LL WORK FOR MANKIND!"

A WEEK LATER, ON APRIL 16, ANNE SAT WITH PETER ON HIS DIVAN.

"I COULD HARDLY TALK."

"MY PLEASURE WAS TOO INTENSE."

MMM...

YOU...

SHE RAN DOWNSTAIRS WITHOUT LOOKING BACK.

MY FIRST KISS!!!!

"I'M STARTING AT A VERY YOUNG AGE," SHE WROTE THE NEXT DAY. "MARGOT WOULD NEVER KISS A BOY UNLESS THERE WAS SOME TALK OF AN ENGAGEMENT OR MARRIAGE."

AND...

"I'M AFRAID OF MYSELF, AFRAID MY LONGING IS MAKING ME YIELD TOO SOON."

AND YET ANNE'S JUDGMENT OF PETER GAVE HER PAUSE.

PETER STILL HAS TOO LITTLE CHARACTER, TOO LITTLE WILLPOWER, TOO LITTLE COURAGE.

WHEN SHE TALKED TO HER FATHER ABOUT HIM...

YOU MUST BE THE ONE TO SHOW RESTRAINT. DON'T GO UPSTAIRS SO OFTEN.

BUT I TRUST HIM. I'LL GO!

ANNE WAS MATURING INTELLECTUALLY, TOO.

I DON'T BELIEVE THE WAR IS SIMPLY THE WORK OF POLITICIANS AND CAPITALISTS...

SHE WOULD LEAD A "DIFFERENT LIFE FROM OTHER GIRLS"...

...AND WOULD NOT BE AN "ORDINARY HOUSEWIFE."

110

111

MAY 11...

MY GREATEST WISH IS TO BE A JOURNALIST, AND LATER ON A FAMOUS WRITER.

The Secret Annex

AFTER THE WAR, I'D LIKE TO PUBLISH A BOOK CALLED "THE SECRET ANNEX."

NINE DAYS LATER, SHE STARTED WRITING HER BOOK, BASED ON HER DIARY, AND LATER BEGAN TO EDIT AND REVISE.

HER RELATIONSHIP WITH PETER CONTINUED AS WELL.

JUST ONE MORE?

BUT SHE STARTED TO PULL BACK A LITTLE.

JUNE 6, 1944, WAS D-DAY, THE LAUNCH OF THE ALLIED INVASION OF WESTERN EUROPE. THEY HEARD RADIO ANNOUNCEMENTS ALL DAY AT THE SECRET ANNEX.

"ENGLISH AND AMERICAN TROOPS ARE ALREADY ENGAGED IN HEAVY COMBAT."

"11,000 PLANES ARE LANDING TROOPS AND BOMBS BEHIND ENEMY LINES."

"4,000 LANDING CRAFT ARE CONTINUALLY ARRIVING."

"I HAVE THE FEELING THAT FRIENDS ARE ON THE WAY," ANNE WROTE.

ON JUNE 12, ANNE CELEBRATED HER FIFTEENTH BIRTHDAY--HER SECOND IN HIDING.

THE HIGH POINT WAS RECEIVING THE BOOK *MARIA THERESIA,* AND THREE SLICES OF CHEESE FROM MR. KUGLER.

PETER HAS DISAPPOINTED ME IN MANY WAYS...WHY DOES HE HIDE HIS INNERMOST SELF AND NEVER ALLOW ME ACCESS?

"I MISS THE REAL THING, AND YET I KNOW IT EXISTS."

THE NEXT DAY, ANNE WROTE AT LENGTH ABOUT HER RELATIONSHIP WITH PETER.

112

THE PAIN OF CHILDBIRTH, SHE HAD READ, WAS MORE THAN A WAR HERO ENDURES.

ANNE ALSO WROTE OF THE INDIGNITY WOMEN FACED AND WONDERED WHY THEY WERE CONSIDERED INFERIOR TO MEN.

MANY WOMEN NOW HAD EDUCATION AND WORK EXPERIENCE.

MANY NATIONS RECOGNIZED EQUAL RIGHTS.

THE 21ST CENTURY WOULD SURELY GRANT WOMEN "RESPECT AND ADMIRATION."

ON AUGUST 1, ANNE FELT "SPLIT IN TWO."

ONE SIDE CONTAINED HER "EXUBERANT CHEERFULNESS...FLIPPANCY...JOY IN LIFE AND APPRECIATION OF 'THE LIGHTER SIDE OF THINGS.'"

HER OTHER SIDE WAS "MUCH PURER, DEEPER, AND FINER."

"NO ONE KNOWS ANNE'S BETTER SIDE," SHE WROTE, "AND THAT'S WHY MOST PEOPLE CAN'T STAND ME."

"MY LIGHTER AND MORE SUPERFICIAL SIDE WILL ALWAYS STEAL A MARCH ON THE DEEPER SIDE..."

"...AND THEREFORE ALWAYS WIN."

"YOU CAN'T IMAGINE HOW OFTEN I'VE TRIED TO PUSH AWAY THIS ANNE, WHICH IS ONLY HALF OF WHAT IS KNOWN AS ANNE..."

"...BUT IT DOESN'T WORK."

ON THE MORNING OF FRIDAY, AUGUST 4, A CALL WAS RECEIVED AT THE OFFICE OF THE SECURITY SERVICE IN AMSTERDAM.

WHAT?

...JEWS ARE HIDING AT 263 PRINSENGRACHT.

TAKE SOME MEN.

YES, SIR.

AT 10:30 THAT MORNING, A CAR PULLED UP...

...AND THREE MEN, LED BY SS OBERSCHARFÜHRER KARL JOSEF SILBERBAUER, EMERGED.

WHO IS IN CHARGE HERE?

I AM.

YOU'RE HIDING JEWS; DON'T DENY IT.

THEY ENTERED THE BUILDING THROUGH THE WAREHOUSE AND CLIMBED THE STAIRS TO THE OFFICE OF VICTOR KUGLER.

IN MOMENTS, THEY WERE IN FRONT OF THE MOVABLE BOOKCASE.

116

117

118

JOHANNES KLEIMAN AND VICTOR KUGLER WERE SENT TO A POLICE TRANSIT CAMP NEAR AMERSFOORT...

...AND ON AUGUST 8, THE EIGHT HIDERS WERE PUT ON A PASSENGER TRAIN TO WESTERBORK, THE TRANSIT CAMP FOR JEWS.

MOVE ALONG AND STAY TOGETHER.

ONCE THEY WERE ABOARD, THE DOORS OF THE TRAIN WERE LOCKED.

ANNE WAS ENTRANCED.

SUMMER...IT'S ALL SO BEAUTIFUL.

OTTO FRANK LATER DECLARED: "ANNE COULD NOT BE TAKEN AWAY FROM THE WINDOW..."

"THERE WERE MEADOWS AND HARVESTED CORNFIELDS. VILLAGES FLEW BY."

119

LOCATED IN THE BLEAK NORTHEAST CORNER OF HOLLAND AND SURROUNDED BY BARBED WIRE, WESTERBORK WAS A HOLDING PLACE FOR PRISONERS, WHO WERE THEN TRANSPORTED TO VARIOUS CONCENTRATION CAMPS ABROAD.

FROM 1942 TO 1945, 107,000 JEWISH MEN, WOMEN, AND CHILDREN PASSED THROUGH WESTERBORK; ONLY 5,200 SURVIVED THE WAR.

BECAUSE THE EIGHT PRISONERS FROM THE SECRET ANNEX HAD RESISTED THE NAZIS BY GOING INTO HIDING, THEY WERE HOUSED IN SPECIAL PUNISHMENT BARRACKS.

WOMEN AND MEN WERE SEPARATED.

BUT IN THE EVENINGS THEY COULD BE TOGETHER.

WE MUST HAVE FAITH THE WAR WILL END SOON.

OTTO SPENT AS MUCH TIME WITH HIS FAMILY AS HE COULD.

THE WOMEN HAD TO OPEN BATTERIES WITH HAMMER AND CHISEL, THEN SEPARATE THE PARTS.

IT WAS FILTHY WORK...

COUGH! COUGH!

THEY STARTED AT 7 A.M. AND WORKED UNTIL 7 P.M.

120

AROUND 70 PEOPLE WERE CROWDED INTO EACH CAR, WITH A SINGLE BUCKET INTO WHICH THEY COULD RELIEVE THEMSELVES.

THE STENCH WAS UNBEARABLE.

"THE TERRIBLE TRIP," OTTO LATER WROTE, "OF THREE DAYS IN A SEALED CATTLE CAR WAS THE LAST TIME I WAS TOGETHER WITH MY FAMILY."

EVERYONE OUT! LEAVE ALL LUGGAGE BEHIND! WOMEN AND CHILDREN TO ONE SIDE, MEN TO THE OTHER!

AFTER THREE DAYS, THEY FINALLY DISEMBARKED AT AUSCHWITZ-BIRKENAU, IN POLAND.

"I SHALL REMEMBER THE LOOK IN MARGOT'S EYES," OTTO SAID LATER, "AS LONG AS I LIVE."

OLDER PEOPLE AND MOTHERS WITH THEIR SMALL CHILDREN WERE TOLD THEY HAD TO TAKE A SHOWER...

...AND SO LINED UP TO ENTER THE GAS CHAMBERS, WHERE THEY WERE ALL KILLED IMMEDIATELY.

THOSE WHO WEREN'T KILLED IMMEDIATELY WERE TATTOOED WITH NUMBERS, HAD TO UNDRESS IN THE PRESENCE OF SS MEN, AND WERE SHAVED BALD BY OTHER PRISONERS.

OTTO, FRITZ PFEFFER, AND HERMANN AND PETER VAN PELS ENDED UP IN THE MEN'S PART OF THE CAMP AT AUSCHWITZ.

THE THREE MEN HAD TO WORK IN A GRAVEL PIT, WHILE PETER WAS FORTUNATE TO BE ASSIGNED TO WORK IN THE CAMP POST OFFICE.

SADLY, HOWEVER, ONE DAY HERMANN VAN PELS BADLY INJURED HIS THUMB AND STAYED BEHIND IN THE BARRACK...

...WHERE HE WAS DISCOVERED BY GUARDS.

HELPLESSLY, OTTO AND PETER WATCHED HIM BEING TAKEN TO THE GAS CHAMBER TO BE MURDERED.

IN OCTOBER, FRITZ PFEFFER WAS DEPORTED TO NEUENGAMME CONCENTRATION CAMP.

BECAUSE OF THE HARD LABOR AND LITTLE FOOD, HE FELL ILL.

FRITZ PFEFFER DIED ON DECEMBER 20, 1944.

ALSO IN OCTOBER, THE HEALTHIEST WOMEN IN AUSCHWITZ WERE SENT TO A MUNITIONS FACTORY IN CZECHOSLOVAKIA.

ANNE, HOWEVER, HAD SCABIES AT THE TIME, AND EDITH AND MARGOT STAYED WITH HER.

SNAPSHOT: BERGEN-BELSEN CONCENTRATION CAMP

CONCENTRATION CAMP

EXTERMINATION CAMP

LOCATED IN THE NORTHWEST SECTION OF GERMANY, BERGEN-BELSEN HAD BEEN ESTABLISHED IN 1940 AS A PRISONER-OF-WAR CAMP FOR 600 FRENCH AND BELGIAN SOLDIERS. IN JULY 1941, 20,000 RUSSIAN PRISONERS WERE INTERNED THERE, IN THE OPEN. ONE YEAR LATER, ABOUT 18,000 HAD DIED.

A SECTION OF THE CAMP IN APRIL 1943 BECAME A "DETENTION CAMP" FOR JEWS SUPPOSEDLY TO BE EXCHANGED FOR GERMAN PRISONERS HELD ABROAD. BY THE TIME THE BRITISH LIBERATED BERGEN-BELSEN ON APRIL 15, 1945, APPROXIMATELY 50,000 INMATES OF THE CONCENTRATION CAMP AND 20,000 RUSSIAN PRISONERS OF WAR HAD DIED THERE.

WHEN HE ARRIVED WITH THE LIBERATING BRITISH UNITS, THE BBC RADIO REPORTER RICHARD DIMBLEBY DESCRIBED WHAT HE SAW:

"HERE, OVER AN ACRE OF GROUND LAY DEAD AND DYING PEOPLE. YOU COULD NOT SEE WHICH WAS WHICH...THE LIVING LAY WITH THEIR HEADS AGAINST THE CORPSES, AND AROUND THEM MOVED THE AWFUL, GHOSTLY PROCESSION OF EMACIATED, AIMLESS PEOPLE, WITH NOTHING TO DO AND NO HOPE OF LIFE, UNABLE TO MOVE OUT OF YOUR WAY, UNABLE TO LOOK AT THE TERRIBLE SIGHTS AROUND THEM."

IN 1944, SS-HAUPTSTÜRMFÜHRER JOSEF KRAMER, WHO HAD WORKED IN MANY CONCENTRATION CAMPS, INCLUDING AUSCHWITZ, BECAME THE COMMANDANT OF BERGEN-BELSEN. NICKNAMED "THE BEAST," HE OVERSAW THE DEATHS OF THOUSANDS. FOR EXAMPLE, HIS SOLUTION FOR OUTBREAKS OF DYSENTERY WAS SIMPLY TO NOT FEED PRISONERS, SO THEY WOULD DIE SOONER.

BY 1945, WHILE KRAMER WAS STILL IN COMMAND, THOUSANDS OF PRISONERS WERE WEAKENED BY STARVATION. THEY EASILY SUCCUMBED TO TYPHOID AND TYPHUS, EPIDEMICS THAT SPREAD WITH TERRIFYING SPEED THROUGH THE OVERCROWDED BARRACKS.

IN EARLY DECEMBER, ANNE AND MARGOT CELEBRATED ST. NICHOLAS DAY, HANUKKAH, AND CHRISTMAS ALL AS ONE HOLIDAY WITH SOME OTHER PRISONERS.

THEY SANG DUTCH SONGS AND ENJOYED THEIR OWN KIND OF "FEAST."

AS JANNY BRILLESLIJPER DESCRIBED, THEY HAD "STALE BREAD...CUT INTO TINY PIECES ON WHICH WE SPREAD ONION AND BOILED CABBAGE."

AUSCHWITZ WAS EVEN COLDER THAN BERGEN-BELSEN. EDITH FRANK HAD GROWN SO WEAK THAT ON JANUARY 6, 1945, SHE DIED FROM ILLNESS AND EXHAUSTION.

IN MID-JANUARY, OTTO AND PETER SEPARATED. THE CAMP WAS EVACUATED; PRISONERS WHO COULD WALK WERE ORDERED ON A MARCH. OTTO TRIED TO CONVINCE PETER TO HIDE IN THE INFIRMARY.

PETER, HIDE HERE...DON'T GO...

I'M YOUNG. I'LL MAKE IT...

AS THE RUSSIANS DREW CLOSER TO AUSCHWITZ, THE NAZIS WANTED TO EVACUATE THE CAMP AND DESTROY THE EVIDENCE OF THEIR CRIMES. THEY BLEW UP GAS CHAMBERS AND CREMATORIA AND TRANSPORTED PRISONERS THEY CONSIDERED ABLE TO WORK ELSEWHERE.

PRISONERS WHO COULD NOT WALK WERE SHOT.

BUT WITH THE RUSSIANS ALMOST AT THE GATES, THE GUARDS FLED.

PETER, MEANWHILE, TRUDGED WITH THOUSANDS OF FELLOW PRISONERS ON THE LONG TREK WEST.

ON JANUARY 27, THE PRISONERS IN AUSCHWITZ WERE LIBERATED BY RUSSIAN FORCES. ONLY 7,650 SURVIVED, INCLUDING OTTO...

...WHO HAD BEEN LYING, WEAK, IN THE INFIRMARY.

IN THE WAREHOUSES, RUSSIAN SOLDIERS FOUND 830,000 WOMEN'S COATS AND DRESSES AND NEARLY 348,000 MEN'S SUITS.

AT MUCH THE SAME TIME, IN BERGEN-BELSEN, ANNE AND MARGOT WERE FREEZING, OFTEN MISSING FOOD FOR DAYS.

BUT ONE DAY DURING THE FIRST MONTHS OF 1945, AUGUSTE VAN PELS, WHO HAD ALSO BEEN DEPORTED FROM AUSCHWITZ TO BERGEN-BELSEN, STOOD NEAR A FENCE SEPARATING TWO PARTS OF THE CAMP WHEN SHE ASKED...

WHO ARE YOU?

IT'S HANNAH GOSLAR...

HANNELI, IT'S ME, MRS. VAN PELS, THE FRIEND OF THE FRANK FAMILY.

I'LL GO GET ANNE!

128

IT WAS A SAD REUNION FOR THE TWO OLD FRIENDS. THEY MET THREE TIMES, ALWAYS WITH THE FENCE BETWEEN THEM.

ANNE! I THOUGHT YOU WERE IN SWITZERLAND!

HOW DO YOU LOOK?

TERRIBLE! MY HEAD IS SHAVEN AND I'VE GROWN SO THIN.

AND MARGOT IS SICK AND FEVERISH.

ANNE ALSO FOUND HER SCHOOLMATE NANNY BLITZ AT THE CAMP.

OH, NANNY, DO YOU REMEMBER WHEN—

THEIR MEMORIES BROUGHT SOME JOY.

IN EARLY FEBRUARY, AUGUSTE VAN PELS WAS FIRST DEPORTED TO THE BUCHENWALD CAMP IN GERMANY AND LATER TO THERESIENSTADT.

SHE WAS MURDERED DURING THAT JOURNEY.

MEANWHILE, MARGOT AND ANNE CONTRACTED TYPHUS, A CONTAGIOUS DISEASE TRANSMITTED BY LICE. THEY HAD HIGH FEVERS AND SUFFERED FROM DELIRIUM.

JANNY BRILLESLIJPER LATER RECORDED THAT ANNE "WAS CRAWLING SO MUCH WITH LICE THAT SHE HAD THROWN AWAY ALL HER CLOTHES."

TIME AND AGAIN, THEY ASKED FOR THE DOOR TO BE SHUT...

PLEASE...PLEASE SHUT THE DOOR.

...TOO WEAK TO SHUT IT THEMSELVES.

JANNY BRILLESLIJPER LATER SAID THAT SOMETIME IN MARCH, "MARGOT FELL OUT OF BED ONTO THE STONE FLOOR...NO LONGER ABLE TO STAND UP."

MARGOT! MARGOT!

SH-SHE'S DEAD!

ANNE DIED SHORTLY AFTER HER SISTER.

ON APRIL 15, JUST WEEKS AFTER ANNE'S AND MARGOT'S TRAGIC DEATHS...

...BRITISH SOLDIERS LIBERATED BERGEN-BELSEN, SHOCKED BY THE CORPSES THAT LAY EVERYWHERE.

AFTER A TERRIBLE JOURNEY, PETER VAN PELS ENDED UP IN MAUTHAUSEN CONCENTRATION CAMP, WHERE HE FELL ILL AND WAS PLACED IN THE INFIRMARY.

HE DIED ON MAY 5, 1945, THE DAY THE CAMP WAS LIBERATED. ONLY ONE OF THE EIGHT HIDERS REMAINED ALIVE.

GERMANY SURRENDERED IN WESTERN EUROPE ON MAY 7, 1945, AND ON THE RUSSIAN FRONT ONE DAY LATER. ON AUGUST 15, 1945, JAPAN SURRENDERED TO END WORLD WAR II, THOUGH THE FORMAL SURRENDER TOOK PLACE ON SEPTEMBER 2.

CHAPTER 10

The Story
Lives On

ARBEIT MACHT FREI

"I HAVE BEEN SAVED BY THE RUSSIANS," OTTO FRANK WROTE TO HIS MOTHER IN SWITZERLAND ON FEBRUARY 23, 1945.

"WHERE EDITH AND THE CHILDREN ARE, I DO NOT KNOW."

ONCE FREE, OTTO STAYED SOME WEEKS IN THE CITY OF OŚWIĘCIM (CALLED AUSCHWITZ BY THE NAZIS), SOME TWO MILES FROM THE CAMP.

IT TOOK HIM FOUR MONTHS TO TRAVEL FROM AUSCHWITZ TO AMSTERDAM BECAUSE OF THE FIGHTING STILL GOING ON IN MANY PARTS OF EUROPE.

OTTO FIRST TRAVELED WITH A GROUP OF SURVIVORS VIA KATOWICE TO ODESSA IN THE U.S.S.R. FROM THERE THEY TOOK A SHIP TO MARSEILLE, FRANCE. AND BY TRAIN AND TRUCK, HE THEN WENT ON TO THE NETHERLANDS.

AMSTERDAM

GERMANY

POLAND

KATOWICE

ODESSA

MARSEILLE

IN KATOWICE, HE MET ROSA DE WINTER, WHO TOLD HIM...

EDITH DIED IN AUSCHWITZ. I'M SO SORRY.

...AND THAT SHE'D LAST SEEN ANNE AND MARGOT BRAVELY FACING THEIR DEPORTATION IN OCTOBER 1944.

ON JUNE 3, 1945, OTTO ARRIVED IN AMSTERDAM AND WENT TO SEE MIEP AND JAN GIES IMMEDIATELY. MIEP RUSHED OUT TO GREET HIM.

MIEP, EDITH IS NOT COMING BACK. BUT I HAVE GREAT HOPE FOR MARGOT AND ANNE.

132

OTTO STAYED WITH MIEP AND JAN, AND WAS GIVEN A BEDROOM OF HIS OWN.

STAY AS LONG AS YOU WANT...

YOU ARE TOO KIND.

HE MET JOHANNES KLEIMAN AND CHARLOTTE KALETTA THAT VERY SAME DAY.

RETURNING TO THE OFFICE THE NEXT DAY TO TAKE HIS PLACE AS THE HEAD OF THE COMPANY...

...HE WAS THRILLED TO MEET VICTOR KUGLER AND BEP VOSKUIJL AGAIN.

OTTO HAD NOT LOST HOPE THAT HE WOULD SEE HIS DAUGHTERS AGAIN...

I AM LOOKING FOR MARGOT AND ANNE FRANK...

SO THE LAST TIME YOU SAW THEM WAS IN FEBRUARY?

YES... SORRY...

THEN ONE DAY...

MIEP...

OTTO HAD MET TWO SURVIVORS FROM BERGEN-BELSEN WHO HAD TOLD HIM THE TERRIBLE TRUTH.

...MARGOT AND ANNE ARE NOT COMING BACK.

134

135

OTTO FRANK'S FIRST ATTEMPTS AT FINDING A PUBLISHER FAILED.

BUT JAN ROMEIN AND HIS WIFE, ANNE, NOTED HISTORIANS, WERE DEEPLY IMPRESSED BY THE DIARY. ON APRIL 3, 1946, JAN'S ARTICLE ABOUT IT APPEARED IN THE DUTCH NEWSPAPER *HET PAROOL*.

"WHEN I HAD FINISHED IT WAS NIGHTTIME AND I WAS ASTONISHED TO FIND THAT THE LIGHTS STILL WORKED, THAT WE STILL HAD BREAD AND TEA..."

"...FOR ME, THIS SEEMINGLY INSIGNIFICANT CHILD'S DIARY... EMBODIES THE REAL HIDEOUSNESS OF FASCISM, MORE SO THAN ALL THE EVIDENCE PRESENTED AT NUREMBERG."

ROMEIN'S ARTICLE WAS WIDELY READ AND PRAISED, AND SEVERAL PUBLISHERS SOON APPROACHED OTTO.

FINALLY! UITGEVERIJ CONTACT WANTS TO PUBLISH ANNE'S DIARY...

OTTO COMPILED AN EDITION OF ANNE'S DIARY, HER REWRITTEN VERSION, AND HER STORIES.

IT WAS PUBLISHED ON JUNE 25, 1947, WITH THE TITLE ANNE HAD WANTED: *HET ACHTERHUIS* (THE SECRET ANNEX).

AROUND THAT TIME, OTTO SPOKE TO THE POLICE ABOUT INVESTIGATING WHO MIGHT HAVE BETRAYED THEM TO THE NAZIS IN 1944.

MR. KLEIMAN HAD WRITTEN TO YOU BEFORE THAT HE BELIEVED A MAN NAMED WILLEM VAN MAAREN, WHO WORKED IN OUR WAREHOUSE, HAD INFORMED THE NAZIS ABOUT US.

WE HAVE RECEIVED THAT LETTER, MR. FRANK.

AND WE WILL BEGIN AN INVESTIGATION.

BUT NO PROOF COULD BE FOUND. NAZI RECORDS HAD BEEN DESTROYED IN AIR RAIDS; OTHERS WERE DESTROYED BY THE NAZIS THEMSELVES. THE INFORMANT WAS NEVER DISCOVERED. IN HIS OLD AGE, OTTO DID NOT WANT TO KNOW ANYMORE: "I CANNOT FORGIVE, BUT I DON'T WANT RETALIATION, I WANT RECONCILIATION."

ONCE PUBLISHED, THE SECRET ANNEX TOOK ON A LIFE OF ITS OWN.

IN 1950, TRANSLATIONS APPEARED IN GERMANY AND FRANCE, AND IN 1952, IN GREAT BRITAIN AND THE UNITED STATES. IT HAS SINCE BEEN TRANSLATED INTO MORE THAN 70 LANGUAGES.

ON NOVEMBER 10, 1953, OTTO MARRIED ELFRIEDE MARKOVITS-GEIRINGER, A SURVIVOR OF AUSCHWITZ LIKE HIMSELF.

THEY HAD MET IN 1945 AS BOTH RETURNED TO AMSTERDAM FROM AUSCHWITZ.

THE DIARY'S SUCCESS CONTINUED.

PLAYWRIGHTS ALBERT HACKETT AND FRANCES GOODRICH CAME TO AMSTERDAM. THEY WERE WRITING A PLAY BASED ON THE DIARY.

THE DIARY OF ANNE FRANK OPENED ON BROADWAY ON OCTOBER 5, 1955, AND RECEIVED EXCELLENT REVIEWS. IT POWERFULLY AFFECTED ITS AUDIENCES, AND RAN FOR 717 PERFORMANCES.

IT WON THE PRESTIGIOUS TONY AWARD AS THE YEAR'S BEST PLAY AND A PULITZER PRIZE FOR ITS TWO PLAYWRIGHTS.

OTTO FRANK COULD NOT BRING HIMSELF TO ATTEND THE OPENING OF THE PLAY.

IN A LETTER TO THE DIRECTOR AND ACTORS, HE WROTE, "THE IDEA THAT MY WIFE AND CHILDREN AS WELL AS I WILL BE PRESENTED ON THE STAGE IS A PAINFUL ONE FOR ME. THEREFORE, IT IS IMPOSSIBLE FOR ME TO COME AND SEE IT."

AND HE NEVER DID...

"INSPIRED THEATRE!"

KERMIT BLOOMGARDEN presents

JOSEPH SCHILDKRAUT

The Diary of Anne Fra

137

A MOVIE BASED ON THE PLAY AND DIRECTED BY THE PROMINENT FILM DIRECTOR GEORGE STEVENS APPEARED IN 1959 TO WIDE ACCLAIM.

IT ALSO WON AN OSCAR FOR THE ACTRESS SHELLEY WINTERS.

THE WORLDWIDE POPULARITY OF THE BOOK, THE PLAY, AND THE FILM CAUSED MANY PEOPLE TO WANT TO VISIT THE SECRET ANNEX.

IN THE EARLY YEARS, VISITORS WERE GIVEN TOURS BY THE FORMER HELPERS.

HOWEVER, IN 1955 THE BUILDING WAS SOLD AND DEMOLITION SEEMED INEVITABLE...

...UNTIL ON MAY 3, 1957, THE ANNE FRANK STICHTING (ANNE FRANK FOUNDATION) WAS SET UP. THREE YEARS LATER, THE ANNEX OFFICIALLY OPENED TO THE PUBLIC AS A MUSEUM CALLED THE ANNE FRANK HOUSE.

OTTO FRANK ORGANIZED INTERNATIONAL YOUTH CONFERENCES ON HUMAN RIGHTS.

AS THE DIARY BECAME POPULAR, EVER MORE PEOPLE WONDERED WHO HAD BETRAYED THOSE IN THE SECRET ANNEX

IN 1963, KARL JOSEF SILBERBAUER, THE MAN WHO HAD LED THE ARREST, WAS FOUND BY THE NAZI HUNTER SIMON WIESENTHAL. SILBERBAUER WAS NOW A POLICEMAN IN VIENNA.

THE ROOMS IN THE MUSEUM WERE LEFT UNFURNISHED. AS OTTO FRANK SAID IN AN INTERVIEW: "DURING THE WAR THEY TOOK EVERYTHING, AND I WANT TO LEAVE IT LIKE THAT."

SILBERBAUER WAS SUSPENDED FROM DUTY AS THE INVESTIGATION OF THE BETRAYAL WAS REOPENED.
BUT HE DID NOT KNOW WHO HAD TURNED IN THE HIDERS.

AFTER A DISCIPLINARY HEARING, SILBERBAUER WAS ALLOWED TO RETURN TO HIS JOB. OTTO FRANK SAW NO REASON FOR THE MAN TO GO PRISON.
"I DON'T WANT IT," HE SAID. "FOR THE REAL CULPRITS WERE THE MEN AT THE TOP."

OTTO AND HIS SECOND WIFE, ELFRIEDE, RECEIVED THOUSANDS OF LETTERS FROM YOUNG READERS OF ANNE'S DIARY FROM ALL OVER THE WORLD. AT THE END OF A REPLY, HE OFTEN WROTE:

"I HOPE ANNE'S BOOK WILL HAVE AN EFFECT ON THE REST OF YOUR LIFE SO THAT, INSOFAR AS IT IS POSSIBLE IN YOUR OWN CIRCUMSTANCES, YOU WILL WORK FOR UNITY AND PEACE."

140

AFTER THE DEATH OF OTTO FRANK, THE STAFF OF THE ANNE FRANK HOUSE CONTINUED TO WORK IN HIS SPIRIT. OVER THE YEARS, MILLIONS OF VISITORS FROM EVERY CORNER OF THE GLOBE HAVE COME TO SEE THE PLACE WHERE ANNE FRANK WROTE HER DIARY, AND TO SEE THE ORIGINAL DIARY ITSELF, WHICH IS THERE ON DISPLAY.

ANNE HAS INDEED BECOME A WORLD-FAMOUS WRITER AND AN INSPIRATION TO MANY.

"When most of the people of my country, Germany, turned into hordes of nationalistic, cruel, anti-Semitic criminals, I had to face the consequences, and though this did hurt me deeply, I realized that Germany was not the world and I left forever."
—OTTO FRANK

- Otto Frank and Edith Holländer marry in Aachen, Germany (May 12, 1925).

- Volume 1 of Adolf Hitler's book *Mein Kampf* is published (July 18, 1925).

- Margot Frank is born in Frankfurt am Main, Germany (February 16, 1926).

- Anne Frank is born in Frankfurt am Main, Germany (June 12, 1929).

- Black Tuesday descends upon the New York Stock Exchange. Prices collapse amid panic selling, and thousands of investors are ruined as a worldwide economic crisis begins (October 29, 1929).

- Adolf Hitler becomes chancellor, the leader of the German government (January 30, 1933).

- Hitler's government organizes a boycott of Jewish shops, doctors, and lawyers. The Nazis say that "real" Germans must not buy from Jews (April 1, 1933).

- Hitler's government bans all other political parties. Now Hitler and his party are in total command. Germany has become a dictatorship (July 14, 1933).

- Otto Frank sets up the Opekta company in Amsterdam (September 15, 1933).

- Alice Frank-Stern, Otto's mother, moves from Frankfurt to Switzerland (October 1933).

- Edith and Margot Frank move to Amsterdam (December 1933).

"In the Netherlands, after those experiences in Germany, it was as if our lives were restored to us. Our children went to school and at least at the beginning our lives proceeded normally. In those days it was possible for us to start over and to feel free."
—OTTO FRANK

- Margot's first day of school in Amsterdam (January 4, 1934).

- Anne Frank is brought to Amsterdam by her uncles Julius and Walter Holländer (February 16, 1934).

- Anne's first day of kindergarten in Amsterdam (April 1934).

- Hitler's government introduces race laws. German Jews have their rights taken away from them. Jews and non-Jews are no longer allowed to get married (September 1935).

- The Nazis destroy Jewish synagogues, shops, and homes throughout Germany. More than 30,000 Jewish men are arrested, and more than 100 Jews are murdered. Later, this night becomes known as Kristallnacht, the "Night of Broken Glass" (November 9, 1938).

- Walter and Julius Holländer immigrate to the Netherlands (Walter in December 1938; Julius in March 1939) and manage to continue their journey to the United States.

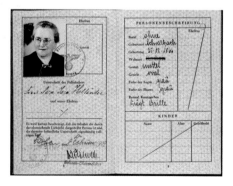

- Fritz Pfeffer and Charlotte Kaletta flee Germany for Amsterdam (December 1938).

- Rosa Holländer-Stern, Anne's grandmother, flees to the Netherlands (March 1939).

- Germany invades Poland. Britain and France declare war on Germany. This is the beginning of the war in Europe (September 1, 1939).

"When I think back to those times during which the occupying forces in Holland introduced regulation after regulation which made life very difficult for us, I have to say that my wife and I did all we could to hide our concerns from the children as far as possible, so that they had a relatively worry-free time."
—OTTO FRANK

- German forces attack and occupy the Netherlands (May 10, 1940). The country surrenders on May 15, and from that date the Netherlands is considered occupied. The royal family and government escape to England.

- Otto Frank's company moves to 263 Prinsengracht in Amsterdam (December 1940).

- Anne and Margot are no longer allowed to go to school with non-Jewish children. They have to go to the Jewish high school in Amsterdam (October 1941).

- Japan bombs the American fleet at Pearl Harbor (December 7, 1941). The next day, America declares war on Japan, as does Britain. Germany supports Japan with a declaration of war against the United States.

- High-ranking Nazis come together in a secret meeting in Berlin. They discuss how to carry out a decision that Hitler had already made in 1941: to kill all 11 million Jews in Europe (January 20, 1942).

- All Jews in the Netherlands age six and older have to wear a star with the word "Jood" (Jew) on their clothes (May 3, 1942).

- Anne's thirteenth birthday. Her favorite present is a diary (June 12, 1942).

- Margot Frank and many other Jews receive a call-up notice. They have to report for a "work camp" in Germany (July 5, 1942).

"Only by adopting a timetable from the start, and each of us having specific duties, were we able to adapt to the situation. In particular, the children needed enough books for reading and studying. Nobody wanted to contemplate how long this voluntary imprisonment might last."

—OTTO FRANK

- The Frank family goes into hiding in the annex at 263 Prinsengracht in Amsterdam (July 6, 1942).

- The van Pels family goes into hiding in the annex (July 13, 1942).

- Fritz Pfeffer goes into hiding in the annex (November 16, 1942).

- The German army surrenders at Stalingrad, Russia, after a battle lasting five months (February 2, 1943).

- Italy surrenders (September 8, 1943).

- D-Day: Allied armies land in northern France as Operation Overlord begins the liberation of Europe (June 6, 1944).

- Anne turns fifteen, her second birthday in the annex (June 12, 1944).

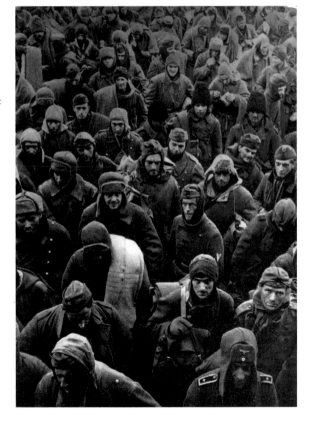

> *"There is still much I cannot talk about, even today. Many things I do not want to talk about anymore. About my feelings, for example, when my family was pulled apart on the ramp in Auschwitz."*
> —OTTO FRANK

- The Frank family, the other people in hiding, and two helpers are betrayed, arrested, and taken to prison (August 4, 1944).

- The people from the hideaways are taken to Westerbork camp (August 8, 1944).

- The people from the hideaways arrive at Auschwitz (September 5–6, 1944).

- Hermann van Pels is killed in the gas chamber (October 1944).

- Anne and Margot are deported from Auschwitz to Bergen-Belsen (October/November 1944).

- Fritz Pfeffer dies in Neuengamme (December 20, 1944).

- Edith Frank dies in Auschwitz (January 6, 1945).

- The Nazis begin the evacuation of Auschwitz. Peter van Pels has to go on a transport. Otto Frank stays behind (January 1945).

- The Russian army liberates Auschwitz, where Otto Frank is being held (January 27, 1945).

- Anne and Margot Frank die in Bergen-Belsen (March 1945).

- Auguste van Pels dies (April 1945).

- Peter van Pels dies in Mauthausen concentration camp (May 5, 1945).

- Europe is liberated from Nazi Germany. This day is known as VE Day, the day of victory in Europe (May 8, 1945).

- Otto Frank returns to Amsterdam. He is the only one of the eight people from the annex to have survived the Holocaust (June 3, 1945).

"Little by little, small groups of survivors returned from the various camps, and from these I tried to find out something about Margot and Anne. Finally I found two sisters who had been together with them in Bergen-Belsen, and who told me about the last sufferings and the death of my children. Both had been so weakened through the deprivations that they had succumbed to the raging typhus. My friends, who had been hoping with me, were now mourning with me."

—OTTO FRANK

- Otto Frank hears that Anne and Margot have died in Bergen-Belsen. Miep hands him Anne's diary (July 18, 1945).

- Leading Nazis are brought to trial in Nuremburg, Germany. Some are sentenced to death, others to long prison sentences (November 20, 1945).

- The first edition of Anne Frank's manuscript, as compiled and edited by Otto Frank, is published in the Netherlands as *Het Achterhuis* (June 25, 1947).

- In 1952, Otto Frank moves to Basel, Switzerland, and marries Elfriede (Fritzi) Markovits (November 10, 1953).

- 263 Prinsengracht opens as a museum, which is named the Anne Frank House (May 3, 1960).

- Otto Frank dies in Basel, Switzerland (August 19, 1980).

SUGGESTIONS FOR FURTHER READING

Anne Frank's diary is available in a translation made by Susan Massotty and published in the United States by Doubleday, a division of Random House, Inc. If you have not read the diary, we urge you to do so: it is one of the most beautiful books to come out of World War II.

Frank, Anne. *Anne Frank's Tales from the Secret Annex*. New York: Bantam, 2003.

Gies, Miep, with Alison Leslie Gold. *Anne Frank Remembered: The Story of the Woman Who Helped to Hide the Frank Family*. New York: Simon and Schuster, 2009.

Gold, Alison Leslie. *Hannah Goslar Remembers: A Childhood Friend of Anne Frank*. London: Bloomsbury, 1999.

Lindwer, Willy. *The Last Seven Months of Anne Frank*. New York: Anchor, 1992.

Müller, Melissa. *Anne Frank: The Biography*. Translated by Rita and Robert Kimber. New York: Picador, 1999.

Prose, Francine. *Anne Frank: The Book, the Life, the Afterlife*. New York: HarperCollins, 2009.

Van Maarsen, Jacqueline. *My Name Is Anne, She Said, Anne Frank: The Memoirs of Anne Frank's Best Friend*. San Francisco: Arcadia Books, 2008.

Westra, Hans. *Inside Anne Frank's House: An Illustrated Journey Through Anne's World*. New York: Overlook Press, 2004.

ONLINE

www.annefrank.org

www.annefrankguide.net

www.annefrank.org/achterhuis

ACKNOWLEDGMENTS

There are so many people we'd like to acknowledge and thank for their help in the creation of this book. First, and as it seems always, our editor and publisher, Thomas LeBien, for his untiring editing and consistent leadership. Enough can never be said for what he has meant to us. And his assistant, Dan Crissman, has always been there to help during this complicated process. Thanks to Eric van Rootselaar, for the cross-section drawing of 263 Prinsengracht on page 51, and to Joris Fiselier, for his corrections of some of the historical maps. Special thanks to Michael Allen for his help in coloring. He was professional, talented, and an important part of the team.

Several people from the Anne Frank House must be specially acknowledged, though everyone there deserves our thanks. Chantal d'Aulnis, publisher, who first brought this project to us, has been a blessing from the moment she first showed us the tiny space in which Anne and her family lived for those tumultuous years. Menno Metselaar, senior editor, cannot be thanked enough for making sure both the story and the art were as authentic and true as was its incredible heroine. He helped make the book better with each comment and suggestion, and brought Anne Frank deeper into our hearts. Teresien de Silva, director of the Anne Frank Collection, did a fantastic job fact-checking our work. Hans Westra, CEO, and Kleis Broekhuizen, COO/CFO, threw their support behind this transatlantic coproduction, offering us gracious hospitality at the museum in Amsterdam and valuable guidance on several visits to the States.

Yes, this book has given us nearly two years of demanding and often difficult work. But it has rewarded us with a glorious adventure that will never be forgotten. And that, perhaps more than anything, is what we'd like to acknowledge.

The research for the drawings was partially based on the "online hiding place," part of the virtual museum offered by the Anne Frank House. In the 3-D online hiding place, visitors can explore the building as it was during the hiding period. Each room offers extra information—for example, notes about the people who lived there and about the things they used in everyday life. You can find it at www.annefrank.org.